CHLOË MOSS

Chloë's first play, *A Day in Dull Armour* (Royal Court), Royal Court's Young Writers' Festival in 2002. Her next play *How Love Is Spelt* (Bush) was awarded a special commendation by the Susan Smith Blackburn Prize. Chloë's other plays include *Christmas is Miles Away* (Manchester Royal Exchange/Bush) and *The Way Home* (Liverpool Everyman). In 2008, Chloë's play *This Wide Night*, produced by Clean Break and presented at Soho Theatre, was awarded the Susan Smith Blackburn Prize, and was revived in autumn 2009. In 2010, her play *Fatal Light* was produced as part of Clean Break's *Charged* season, a collection of plays written about women in the criminal justice system. Chloë also writes for television and radio.

Other Titles in this Series

Chloë Moss

THE
GATEKEEPER

NICK HERN BOOKS
London
www.nickhernbooks.co.uk

A Nick Hern Book

The Gatekeeper first published in Great Britain as a paperback original in 2012 by Nick Hern Books Limited, 14 Larden Road, London W3 7ST

The Gatekeeper copyright © 2012 Chloë Moss

Chloë Moss has asserted her right to be identified as the author of this work

Cover image: Dragonfly Design www.dragonfly-design.co.uk
Original cover concept: Royal Exchange Theatre
Cover design: Ned Hoste, 2H

Typeset by Nick Hern Books, London
Printed in the UK by Mimeo Ltd, Huntingdon, Cambridgeshire PE29 6XX

A CIP catalogue record for this book is available from the British Library

ISBN   978 1 84842 260 5

For Tim

The Gatekeeper was first performed at the Royal Exchange
Theatre, Manchester, on 8 February 2012, with the following
cast:

ANGELA	Helen Carter
STACEY	Kate Coogan
JULIA	Tricia Kelly
ROB	Nick Moss
MIKE	Ian Redford

Director	Tessa Walker
Designer	Chloe Lamford
Lighting	Richard Owen
Sound Designer	Steve Brown
Assistant Director	Anna Marsland
Fight Director	Alison De Burgh

8

Characters

STACEY, *thirty-five*

JULIA, *Stacey's mother, sixty-four*

MIKE, *Stacey's father, sixty-five*

ANGELA, *thirty-four*

ROB, *Stacey's brother, thirty-eight*

Note on the Text

A forward slash in the text (/) indicates a character changing tack.

A dash in the text (–) indicates another character interrupting, or overlapping speech.

Special thanks to

Tessa Walker, Mel Kenyon, Sarah Frankcom, Polly Jerrold and all at the Royal Exchange, Patricia Moss, Ken Moss, Nick Moss and Colette Kane. Also, Roxana Silbert, Pippa Hill, Nina Steiger, Kate Ashfield, Keith Barron, Claire-Louise Cordwell and Alison Steadman.

This text went to press before the end of rehearsals and so may differ slightly from the play as performed.

ONE

A holiday cottage. STACEY *paces the living room, on her phone. She is wearing a long, expensive coat, there's a small suitcase on wheels by the door.*

STACEY. Claire. (*Beat.*) Claire, Claire, Claire, just / I told you. I told you ten times. I emailed you. I left a note on your desk. How many ways do you want me to. (*Beat.*) Tell them to hold it. (*Beat.*) They can't. They're not allowed. (*Beat.*) They always say that. They always say that's the final print deadline but there's *always* more time. It's a fucking game. So play the game and tell them we'll pull it if they don't change it. Don't worry about the client, just do it. Now. (*Beat.*) Do you want to keep your job? Claire? Do you want to… (*Beat.*) Then fucking do it. *Now.*

STACEY *slumps down onto the couch, putting her head in her hands. As she does so,* JULIA *springs up from behind the couch, followed by a reluctant* MIKE.

JULIA. Surprise.

STACEY. Jesus.

STACEY *jumps up, startled.* JULIA *comes round to hug her.*

JULIA. Sorry, sorry. We didn't mean to give you the frights.

MIKE. We came early. It was your mother's idea. (*Beat.*) Is everything alright?

STACEY. Yes. Yeah, sorry that was just a… thing. Work thing. It's nothing.

JULIA. Was it Claire?

Beat.

STACEY. Yeah.

JULIA. She's a lovely girl, Claire. Do you remember Claire, Mike? Little pretty blonde one.

STACEY. How did you get in?

JULIA. I phoned the woman on the brochure and explained. She wasn't as friendly on the phone as she was face to face. She probably saw us and thought, 'Well, they don't look very suspicious.' (*Beat.*) I thought it might be nice. To get here and find us waiting.

MIKE *loosens his tie and puts a hand to his forehead.*

Oh, Christ, what's the matter?

MIKE. I'm hot, what d'you think the matter is? (*Beat.*) Sweating like a whore in church.

JULIA. For God's sake.

MIKE *looks around the room.*

MIKE. It is *exactly* the same, isn't it?

STACEY. I know. Look, same couch, do you remember that couch? That couch must be, what? Twenty years old?

MIKE. More. When did we come here, Julia?

JULIA. Eighty-four and eighty-six. We were all booked for eighty-five but your mother had a stroke. (*Touching the sofa.*) I hope it gets a regular clean. It's a shame about David.

STACEY. He's in the middle of a big project so he needs to stay at home. Concentrate. It's all go for him at the moment, for both of us really. It was hard enough getting away myself.

MIKE. Good to be busy.

STACEY. Exactly.

JULIA. It's good to be busy but not when it's eating into your weekends.

STACEY. Weekends are not in our vocab at the minute, Mum.

JULIA. I'm sure that can't be good for you.

MIKE. The only place success comes before work is…

STACEY. In the dictionary.

JULIA. I was looking forward to seeing him.

MIKE. We'll come up and stay.

JULIA. I just got geared up, that's all. I felt… excited.

MIKE. Leave it, will you, Julia. For Christ's sake. The man can't make it. He's got bigger fish to fry. Move on. (*Looking around the room.*) Needs some work doing.

JULIA. You need some work doing.

MIKE. What does that even bloody mean, Julia?

STACEY. I've got some walks planned for us. Have you seen how beautiful it is? I forgot how beautiful it is. I was driving along before through Grasmere and I felt my shoulders just drop.

MIKE. Oh, Christ, yeah, beautiful part of the world.

STACEY. Isn't it? You get so used to rushing around, don't you? Especially with work being so manic –

MIKE. Manic is good.

STACEY. Yeah, of course –

JULIA. Manic is not good. I read this article in the *Express* last week about high-pressured jobs and heart attacks –

MIKE (*looks at his watch*). Four minutes, that might be a record.

JULIA. It's affecting more and more women, apparently. They did a double-page spread. About five of them had a makeover, all much younger than you'd expect. Oldest was probably, I dunno… fifty. She had very big hips and they put her in this skirt that was cut on the bias. That is not a flattering look for a pear-shaped woman. Although, funnily enough, they're supposed to be the least likely to have a coronary because they carry all their fat around their hips. Apples are the worst. (*To* MIKE.) Your mother was a typical apple.

MIKE. Is there a point to this, Julia?

JULIA. The point is, they all blamed their jobs.

STACEY. I'm not gonna have a heart attack, Mum.

JULIA. Nobody *thinks* they're going to have a heart attack.

STACEY. Well, I'm here, I'm not at work and I'm suggesting that we go on lots of big walks in the fresh air. So that's a start, hey?

JULIA. I haven't brought my boots.

MIKE. It's the Lake District, woman. Bloody walking capital of the… England and you're gonna be tottering around in those things.

JULIA. I don't totter. They're quite supportive.

MIKE. I thought we could go up to Loughrigg Fell. It's only a couple of miles. We can all go in the morning maybe then have lunch in Skelwith Bridge.

JULIA. Lovely. Now, I did see rain forecast.

STACEY. It's not going to rain.

JULIA. I'm only saying what I read in the paper.

STACEY (*holds up an iPhone*). I've checked on this, it's going to be dry the whole weekend. It's not going to rain.

JULIA. Intermittent heavy showers, I read.

STACEY. It won't rain.

JULIA. Might brighten up in the morning but late afternoon both days are a write-off apparently.

Beat.

STACEY. Have you been upstairs yet?

MIKE. Yes, we were going to leave our bags in the hall but your mother wouldn't entertain it, said it'd spoil 'The Surprise'. The surprise of us arriving slightly earlier than expected.

Muggins here had to lug the bloody lot up the stairs and hide them in the airing cupboard.

STACEY. You can have any room you like. I thought the front one because it's the biggest but then the one at the back's got the nicest view, hasn't it? You can see right over to Morecambe. (*Beat.*) Have a look anyway, can't you? See what you fancy.

JULIA. You know what your father's like. He'll sleep on a washing line. He doesn't care, do you? I don't care either to be honest. As long as it's not draughty.

MIKE. What would you know about being cold? Central heating on morning, noon and night. I'm surprised me insides haven't shrivelled up like dried fruit. I woke up last night and me tongue was welded to the roof of me mouth. Thought I'd had a fucking stroke.

JULIA. Do you have to, Michael? Do you honestly have to? It's Stacey's birthday. Anyway, you wouldn't get a dry mouth if you took a glass of water up with you. Half a bottle of scotch a night, you're going to get more than a dry mouth, you'll get bloody gout. (*Beat.*) Do you want your present, Stace?

MIKE. Let her get her coat off.

STACEY. It isn't my birthday for a fortnight.

JULIA. I know but we're *celebrating* your birthday now, aren't we? And I always post it. I haven't actually given you a present in years. Not face to face.

   JULIA *and* MIKE *take their coats off and sit down on the couch.* JULIA *takes a wrapped present out of her bag and places it on her lap.*

MIKE. The traffic was a disgrace.

JULIA. It's the weekend, isn't it? People are going places. I don't mind. I do a crossword. Read... put the radio on. You make a choice, don't you? 'Give peace and you will feel peaceful.'

MIKE. Oh, don't start with that, for Christ's sake.

JULIA. 'Thought for the Day' in the newspaper, Stace. I cut them out and collect them. Yesterday's was 'Climbing is not about conquering the rock; it is about conquering yourself.' I like that one even though I'm not quite sure what it means. But that's half the fun sometimes. I cut them out and stick them on the fridge. They've got this offer at the moment. You can send away for a little book of them. One ninety-nine and four coupons. I might do that but to be honest there's something very satisfying about waiting each day for a new one. I do my bits around the house then I settle down with a coffee. I think if I got the book I'd probably just rattle through the whole lot in one go and then that'd be it, wouldn't it? (*Beat.*) Nothing to look forward to.

Silence.

Anyway, you can get het up or you can just relax. Not a thing in the world you can do about traffic jams, is there?

MIKE *looks at* JULIA *incredulously.*

MIKE. Says the woman who's never driven in her life. It's easy to relax when you're sat on your arse, isn't it?

JULIA. I'm not sat on my arse. I'm navigating.

MIKE. Julia, you couldn't navigate your way out of the porch.

STACEY*'s mobile rings.*

STACEY. 'Scuse me for a sec.

STACEY *leaves the room, shutting the door behind her. Muffled shouting can be heard.*

This is fucking child's play, Claire. Basic skills… Tell them you don't give a shit… Tell them to… Yes… I don't want to hear from you again until it's fucking sorted, okay?

MIKE *and* JULIA *sit in complete silence.* STACEY *returns a few moments later.*

Shall we have a drink? Let's have a drink. Glass of wine? G and T?

JULIA (*laughing*). Oooh!

MIKE. Bit early, isn't it?

JULIA. Mike, it's a party.

STACEY *goes into the kitchen. She returns carrying a crate of assorted drinks.*

I'll be on my back trying to make my way through that.

MIKE. You don't *have* to drink it all, Julia. There is such a thing as restraint.

JULIA. It's a special weekend. The four of us together.

STACEY *stops.*

MIKE. She's invited Robert.

JULIA *whacks* MIKE *on the arm.*

JULIA. It was supposed to be a surprise.

MIKE. You just bloody said it yourself, 'the four of us'. What is it with and you surprises anyway? It's like living with Jeremy fucking Beadle.

JULIA. Oh, Mike, don't be disgusting, the man's dead.

Beat.

STACEY. Is he coming?

MIKE. Jeremy Beadle? Probably, knowing her.

MIKE *laughs at his own joke.* STACEY *is still absorbing the news.*

STACEY. Rob? Is Rob coming?

JULIA. Yes.

MIKE. He *says* he's coming.

STACEY. When did you speak to him?

JULIA. The other week. He called. Straight off the plane apparently. He's got so much to tell us, hasn't he? Travelling all around… Where's he been again?

STACEY. Thailand.

JULIA. Thailand. (*Beat.*) You two with your lives, I don't know. He's everso excited.

MIKE. Don't hold your breath.

JULIA. What's that supposed to mean?

MIKE. People say they're going to do things. They say they're going to do things and then they don't do them. It happens all the time. Especially where Robert's concerned.

STACEY. But he says he's coming?

MIKE. He *says* he's coming.

JULIA. He's coming. He can't wait. (*Beat.*) Isn't that lovely? All four of us together.

Beat.

STACEY. Lovely.

JULIA. When was the last time that happened? *Years.*

MIKE. My sixtieth.

JULIA. Your sixtieth. It was, wasn't it?

MIKE. Yes. It was. And what a wonderful time we had.

Silence.

STACEY. Shall I open a bottle of red?

JULIA. 'A bottle of red.' I love how they say things in London. You don't say open a bottle of red *wine*, do you? It's just 'a bottle of red'.

STACEY *opens a bottle of wine, hands the glasses round.*

STACEY. Cheers.

JULIA. Eyes, Mike.

MIKE *lifts his glass and purposefully clinks it against* JULIA*'s, staring into her eyes. She stares back.*

MIKE. So he's busy then? David? Good man.

JULIA. He works too hard. They should give him some time off.

STACEY. His choice.

MIKE. Healthy work ethic never killed anyone. You reap what you sow. Companies are too scared to really crack the whip these days. I read the other day about a place in London with a slide. A *slide*. In the office. Grown men and women sliding down a bloody… slide. I felt like writing in. They've been voted the 'most *fun* company to work for'. Since when was work supposed to be 'fun', eh? What the hell's that all about?

STACEY. To make sure people get on. Increase productivity.

MIKE. I worked alongside Jeffrey Holmes for twenty years. Detested the man, he was a fuckin' gobshite. *Fun* was the last thing we had, but did it affect our work? Did it buggery.

JULIA. Stacey has fun, don't you?

STACEY.…

MIKE. She doesn't have *fun*, Julia. There's a difference between being passionate about your career and having *fun*. (*Beat*.) Richard from next-door-but-one, his son works in an office. In a 'team'. Last weekend they went away to Wales for a 'team-building trip'. They did 'team-building' exercises. Richard's son had to… Well, they all had to… climb up a sort of pole while attached to a harness. At the top of the pole there's this sort of wobbling platform just big enough to sit on and you have to try and stay on it for as long as possible. If you fall, your 'team members' catch you. (*Beat*.) So Richard's son –

JULIA. Daniel.

MIKE. Daniel's very good at this because he's a sporty type, isn't he?

JULIA. He's big-built, yes. Not the tallest of chaps but he's very broad-shouldered –

MIKE. Very fit and young and all that and it isn't a problem and he quite enjoys it apparently.

JULIA. He likes a challenge.

MIKE. Do *you* want to tell the story?

JULIA. I don't know it, how could I tell it?

   Beat.

MIKE. So. There's the pole – thing – at the top to sit on…
Everyone waits around the bottom in case you fall, but the
idea is that it doesn't matter if you *do* fall because as I said,
your 'team members' catch you. So next up is a larger lady
and Richard said that it was obvious that she didn't want to
do it –

JULIA. Was Richard there?

MIKE. Why would Richard be there, Julia?

JULIA. How did he know it was obvious she didn't want to do
it then?

MIKE. Because his son –

JULIA. Daniel.

MIKE. *Daniel* said it was obvious. But they had this very
bombastic team leader apparently. Anyway, she makes her
way up, this big woman, and she's clearly getting more and
more distressed about the whole thing but she makes it to
the wobbly platform at the top and everyone cheers.
Anyway, it's all a bit premature and she falls. And nobody
catches her.

STACEY. But she was on a harness?

MIKE. She was on a harness, yeah, but it's not much fucking
fun, is it? Smacking against the side of a ruddy huge pole.
The harness is just back-up.

JULIA. You wouldn't get me up a pole.

MIKE. I wouldn't catch you. Not if you'd gone up for that
reason. Team-building. I'm glad I'm out of it all if that's
the way it's going. These young ones with their bloody
ideas. Lad started at our place about a year before I retired,

I say 'lad' for a reason – little string of piss, shaved twice a
week. Luke Taylor. He says, 'In my last company…'
Probably fuckin' Tumble Tots. I thought of that afterwards,
I wish I'd said it at the time, anyway he says, 'We had
duvet days.' Duvet days. (*Beat.*) You just ring up and say
you can't be bothered coming in. You're staying in bed.
(*Beat.*) That's why it's all going to pot, isn't it? Eh?
Bollocks like that. It's mad.

JULIA. David's not mad, is he, Stacey?

MIKE. He doesn't go in for all that though, does he?

STACEY. He does actually.

MIKE. Only because he has to. They force them. It's bloody
ridiculous.

STACEY. He quite enjoys it. Lets off a bit of steam. He went on
one a couple of months ago to Wiltshire, tore round the
countryside all day on an Apache off-road racer.

MIKE. Oh, well, that's different. An Apache off-road racer. That
is a bit of fun. Not all this US bonding bullshit. That's about
saying, 'You work hard. We *appreciate* you.'

JULIA. Do they appreciate him then, Stace? You don't mind
working Saturdays if they appreciate you, do you?

STACEY. I didn't tell you about his bonus, did I? Did I tell you
about his bonus?

JULIA. I don't think you did. We would have remembered,
wouldn't we?

STACEY. Few weeks before –

JULIA. I hope you haven't. I should have sent a card.

MIKE. Let her tell the bloody story.

STACEY. Few weeks before Christmas he gets called into
Clive's – that's his boss – he gets called into the office. For a
'chat' –

MIKE. Oh, sweet Jesus.

STACEY. He goes in and David sits down and his boss does this big preamble about what a bad year it's been, how it's affecting bonuses, all that. (*Beat.*) I've told you about him before, haven't I? Clive. David's boss? He's very... dour. Straightforward. Straight to the point about things, so in this situation –

MIKE. Oh, Christ, yeah –

STACEY. So he reaches into his drawer and gets something out but David can't see it properly because he's sort of holding it under the desk, out of view. Then, he puts it on the desk and it's a box of Quality Street and he apologises for it not being what David was probably expecting –

JULIA. Still, it's a nice thought.

STACEY. David's going to pieces now –

MIKE. Well, he's so straightforward, Clive.

JULIA (*to* MIKE). Why can you interrupt but I can't?

MIKE (*finger to his lips*). Ssshh.

STACEY. David goes to pick the box up. He just wants to get out of there as fast as he can.

MIKE. Save face. Absolutely.

STACEY. But he picks it up and it's *heavy*. Like... too heavy for chocolates. He opens it and inside there's this wad of cash. Guess how much?

MIKE. Five hundred.

STACEY. Higher.

MIKE. Grand.

STACEY *shakes her head.*

Two grand.

STACEY. Keep going.

MIKE. You are tonking my chain.

STACEY. Ten. Grand.

MIKE. Ten thousand?

JULIA. Pounds?

MIKE. Krona. What d'you bloody think, Julia?

STACEY. Highest in his team. In the company probably.

JULIA. Were the Quality Street in there too?

STACEY. No, Mum.

JULIA. Aww.

MIKE. Good lad. Here's to David then, eh?

JULIA. It's Stacey's birthday.

MIKE. And Stace. Of course.

JULIA. To David. And Stacey. (*Beat.*) Do you feel like your present yet, Stace?

    JULIA *holds the present up triumphantly.*

    I've kept the receipt. (*Beat.*) You can take it back. I promise I won't be in the slightest bit offended.

    STACEY *unwraps the present and holds it up, it's a garish, pink-lace top. She takes it in, trying to think of something to say.* JULIA *watches expectantly.*

STACEY. It's lovely.

JULIA. You can take it back.

STACEY. I don't want to take it back.

JULIA. You've got twenty-eight days. (*Beat.*) Twenty-three now actually because I got it last Thursday but you can take it to any branch. I checked with the woman. Her name's Lisa if you need it.

STACEY. It's lovely. Really nice… colour.

    STACEY *holds it up against herself.*

JULIA. Remember when you were little? *Everything* had to be pink. What was her room like, Mike?

MIKE. Pink.

JULIA. Walls, ceiling, lampshades, carpet, bedclothes, dressing table –

MIKE. We've got the idea.

STACEY *folds the top up carefully and places it on the side of the chair.*

JULIA. It might not fit. You look tiny.

STACEY. I'll try it on in a bit. I could swap it for a smaller size if it is.

JULIA. You can't. You can take it back and get a credit note but you can't get a different size. It was all end-of-line stuff. (*Beat.*) I didn't get it because it was in the sale. It wasn't even marked down that much. Twenty per cent at Debenhams. I would've got it regardless. (*Beat.*) I've got the receipt in my purse. Where's my purse?

STACEY. I don't want to take it back, Mum.

JULIA. It's in my handbag. Where's my handbag? Airing cupboard.

MIKE. Course.

JULIA *leaves.*

So am I going to have to get on me knees and beg then?

MIKE *holds his arms out.* STACEY *stands and hugs him tightly.*

That's better. How are you, princess?

STACEY. I'm fine. Everything's great. Really, yeah. Fine. (*Beat.*) What about you? How are you finding it?

MIKE. Very… pleasant. You picked a good spot. Nice idea to come back here. Memories and all that.

STACEY. Retirement, I meant. (*Beat.*) Are you enjoying being retired?

MIKE. What's not to enjoy? Free man. All the time in the world on me hands. No stress. Can't be doing with stress. Not at my age. (*Beat.*) Be nice for your mum if you came and saw us a bit more often. I know you're busy. Busy life. You and David. Pair of you. But still.

STACEY. I know. I'm sorry.

MIKE. Don't apologise to me. I understand it... I just think your mum could do with a bit more. She's on these pills for her nerves. I know it's a hassle. Better things to do.

STACEY. It's not a hassle.

MIKE. Richard, next-door-but-one. His son... Three kids. Finance director... Hell of a lot of pressure. Can't stay away. Six-hour drive but he makes it up at least once a month. Parks his Maserati outside our house. I don't mind, he always asks. He's had bucket seats put in. Bit tacky.

STACEY. It's been a bit difficult lately. Getting away.

MIKE. I think it's unhealthy. Once a month. He's a grown man, family of his own to look after. But he makes that choice and they really appreciate it. Richard and Norma. (*Beat.*) They go fishing. Richard and his son, not Richard and Norma. I took Rob fishing once. Bloody disaster, he wouldn't touch the maggots. I gave him gloves but he wasn't having any of it. Didn't see much point after that. If you can't handle a maggot how you going to cope with a seven-pound rainbow trout? (*Beat.*) Uncle Dennis died.

STACEY. I know. I'm sorry. I liked Uncle Dennis.

MIKE. Funeral wasn't bad. I was dreading it. All that small talk. (*Beat.*) But it was alright as it goes. Nigel wasn't there. Which was a result. Uncle Chris *was* there but that wasn't so bad... he's mellowed. You know what he's like... first to put his hand in his pocket. And keep it there. He got a round in though. Could've bowled me over with a feather.

STACEY. How's Auntie Jean?

MIKE. Not great. Quite surprising, to be honest. Spends her whole life trying to flog the poor sod to death then when he goes, she's beside herself. (*Beat.*) They all asked after you. Your mother told them you were having a small operation. (*Beat.*) Wisdom teeth, in case you speak to anyone.

STACEY. I sent her a card. (*Beat.*) I will go and see her though. When I'm up.

MIKE. It's boring, I know. Keeping up to speed with a load of old dinosaurs.

STACEY. It's not boring.

MIKE. It is boring. *They're* boring. But it's family. You might not care but you can at least pretend. Make an effort.

STACEY. I know. It's important.

MIKE. It is important. Boring but important. (*Beat.*) I got your email.

Beat.

STACEY. We don't have to talk about it now. You've only just got through the door.

MIKE. I didn't reply because there didn't seem much point, coming here a couple of days later. Seeing you.

STACEY. Course, yeah, but honestly let's not / Not now. I haven't seen you for so –

MIKE. This *opportunity*, as you're calling it.

Pause.

STACEY. I don't want you to think / It's an *investment.* Really. It wouldn't be about helping me out of a rut –

MIKE. You never mentioned a rut.

STACEY. There isn't a rut. That's what I mean. It's not about a *rut.*

MIKE. But you need money.

STACEY. That's a *part* of it yes but just as much as that, more than that. I just wanted some advice. Things are good. (*Beat.*) But it hasn't been easy.

MIKE. It won't have been easy. It's not *meant* to be easy. That's the whole point.

STACEY. Exactly.

MIKE. No man. Or female. (*Beat.*) Has ever made it to the top without a hell of a fucking struggle on the way.

STACEY. I'm not struggling, it's just been a bit... *uphill*. Recently.

MIKE. Uphill?

STACEY. There's nothing to worry about.

MIKE. Should I be worrying?

STACEY. There's *nothing* to worry about.

MIKE. I'm an old man, Stacey. I can't afford to be taking risks.

STACEY. God. Of course / Dad. D'you *honestly* –

MIKE. I haven't mentioned anything to your mother. You know what she's like.

STACEY. You know I'm not coming to you because you're my dad? It's because I think you're the best person to help.

MIKE. Not David?

STACEY. Not David, no –

MIKE. No. I understand.

Silence.

STACEY. I want you to think about it. There's no rush. We shouldn't even talk about it now. (*Beat.*) I just want us to have a nice weekend. Being... together.

JULIA *enters clutching the receipt.*

JULIA. Twenty-two days. My mistake. It's because I got my doctor's appointment muddled. I thought I had it for the Friday but it was actually for the Thursday but I couldn't seem to get that out of my head, even when I went on the Thursday, I kept thinking it was Friday, didn't I?

MIKE. You did.

JULIA. And because I went into town the day before my doctor's appointment to get your present I've got it in my head that it was a Thursday when actually it was the Wednesday. It's messed up my whole week. (*Holding the receipt out to* STACEY.) Here you go, keep it somewhere safe.

MIKE *throws his paper down onto the floor.*

I hope you're going to pick that up. There's a paper rack there, put it in the paper rack.

MIKE. When I get up.

JULIA. When are you getting up?

MIKE. When I need a piss.

JULIA. I'm so sorry about this, Stacey.

MIKE *stands. He puts the paper in the rack and goes to the door.*

Where are you going?

MIKE. For a piss.

MIKE *leaves.*

JULIA. He's been like this the whole way down.

STACEY. Mum, it's fine.

JULIA. It's not fine. Not on your birthday.

STACEY. It's not my birthday.

JULIA. He's depressed. Since he retired. He won't admit it but he is. He's unbearable at times. I wish he'd get a hobby. I bought him some crayons last week, you wet them and they turn into watercolours. He just threw them in the bin. (*Beat.*) It's good for him, this… A little break. (*Beat.*) Do you think those books are real?

STACEY. Why wouldn't they be real?

JULIA. They look like those… video cases your Auntie Jean used to keep in the living room. I've noticed that they do it in the The Lion and Unicorn at home. I was in there with your dad the other month and he's off talking about shares and I think I might have a little look at *Wuthering Heights* so I pull at it and the whole row comes out. They're just those fake spines glued onto boxes. (*Beat.*) I suppose people might steal them otherwise. It's terribly sad.

JULIA *stands and goes over to the bookshelf. She pulls a book off and lets out a little surprised shriek. She studies it.*

Oh, lovely. I'll have a read of this. Do you think that's allowed?

STACEY. Of course. It's a book. It's meant to be read.

The door opens and MIKE *enters.*

JULIA. Look at all the books, Mike.

MIKE. Are they real?

JULIA. Of course they're bloody real. I might take one up.

MIKE. Stacey and I were thinking of a quick stroll. Stretch our legs. (*Beat.*) Weren't we?

STACEY. Yes. Yeah… just a potter.

MIKE. You stay here, love. Have a read.

JULIA. Stace, you don't mind, do you?

STACEY. Mum, I just want you to relax. Both of you. That's what you're here for, isn't it?

MIKE *holds the door for* STACEY.

JULIA *takes the book and the bottle of wine and leaves.*

TWO

It's raining hard outside. STACEY *and* ANGELA *stand opposite each other, staring.* ANGELA *is wet through. She bursts out laughing.* STACEY *joins in nervously.*

ANGELA. You haven't changed a bit.

STACEY. No? God, I think –

ANGELA. I mean you have obviously. You look a lot older but like not… *different*, d'you know what I mean?

STACEY *nods, goes to speak.*

Remember Becky Collins?

STACEY. Yeah –

ANGELA. She comes in the shop sometimes and I swear to God you'd walk past that girl in the street and you wouldn't think for a second it's the same person. And it's not just the weight. It's like her features have shifted. Her nose is *completely* different. She's not had any work done. Or at least I hope she hasn't cos I tell you what, I'd want me money back. (*Beat.*) Do you think it's kids that does that?

STACEY. I don't know.

ANGELA. Have you got kids?

STACEY. No. No kids.

ANGELA. See. I knew that. I could tell. Although saying that, I haven't got any and I think I've changed *a hell* of a lot.

STACEY. You haven't.

ANGELA. Oh, I have. I was looking at some photos the other day and I actually didn't recognise meself in a couple.

STACEY. I recognised you straight away. You look great.

ANGELA. Kidding, aren't you? Can I get a towel?

STACEY. Oh, God, of course, you're drenched, sorry.

STACEY gets a tea towel and hands it to ANGELA who starts to dry her hair with it.

ANGELA. Ta.

STACEY. They said it was going to stay dry.

ANGELA. You haven't got a mirror as well, have you?

STACEY rummages in her bag and pulls out a small compact mirror.

Nice one.

ANGELA looks in the mirror, her eye make-up is streaked across her face.

Oh, frigging hell.

ANGELA fixes her make-up. STACEY stares, not quite sure what to do.

So, what you up to then?

STACEY....

ANGELA dabs on some lip gloss and hands the compact back to STACEY.

ANGELA. Life. (*Beat.*) Married?

STACEY. I live with someone.

ANGELA. A man?

Beat.

STACEY. Yeah, yeah, yeah. My boyfriend. My '*fella*'. David. He's brilliant. We've been together since uni.

ANGELA. No.

STACEY. Fifteen years. (*Beat.*) He's brilliant.

ANGELA. He'd have to be, wouldn't he? Fifteen years.

STACEY. He's a sales director.

ANGELA. Sound. (*Beat*.) Nice place.

STACEY. We used to come here when me and Rob were little.

ANGELA. Nothing ever matches in posh houses, does it? You'd think with all that money they could afford to get a bit of a theme going. (*Beat*.) I don't mind it. I quite like it.

Silence. ANGELA *picks up a packet of cigarettes from the kitchen table and hands it to* STACEY.

STACEY. I don't smoke.

ANGELA. Given up? Well done.

STACEY. Hardly even started really.

ANGELA. My bad influence, eh?

STACEY. Something like that.

ANGELA. I knocked it on the head last year but I have lapses. Worse than smack, innit? Not that I'd know, don't worry. (*Beat*.) You don't still live up there then?

STACEY. I'm based in London now.

ANGELA. 'Based.'

STACEY *laughs nervously again*.

You don't half sound posh. Like, you were posh before but now it's even worse. Not worse, sorry. You've got a lovely voice. Can't *really* pinpoint where you're from. Probably quite useful that though, isn't it? Saves you getting wotsit… pigeon-holed.

Beat.

STACEY. This is *such* a nice surprise.

ANGELA. Didn't he mention me?

STACEY. I'm sure he would have, if we'd spoken. We haven't spoken for a while. I mean, we're speaking, we're not not speaking, we just haven't spoken. Lately. (*Beat*.) He's been away –

ANGELA. Thailand.

Beat.

STACEY. Yes.

ANGELA. I find that dead attractive, y'know? He's got that 'man of the world' thing going on, hasn't he? A free spirit.

STACEY. I suppose so. We're quite different.

ANGELA. You are very different.

STACEY. How… long has it –

ANGELA. Not long. Couple of months.

Beat.

STACEY. And it's… going well?

ANGELA. Early days but yeah I like him. I like his… vibe, d'you know what I mean?

STACEY *has no idea what* ANGELA *means.* ANGELA *stares at her.*

Oh my God, if there was an opposite of peas in a pod –

STACEY. Chalk and cheese.

ANGELA. Chalk and cheese, massively. Hilarious.

ANGELA *laughs.* STACEY *joins in, a nervous, awkward laugh.*

STACEY. Can I get you a drink? We should do a toast or something.

ANGELA. Fuck it, yeah, I'll have a vodka and orange. It's the weekend, eh?

STACEY *starts to prepare the drinks.*

We haven't come empty-handed. Rob's gone the shop. If there is a shop round here. He just set off. He does that, doesn't he? He just fucking sets off. I need to know where I'm going. Do you drive, Stacey?

STACEY. Yeah.

ANGELA. I don't. I pretend it's for the environment but I just can't be arsed.

STACEY hands ANGELA a drink.

I looked for you on Facebook.

STACEY. I don't bother with Facebook.

ANGELA. No, I didn't think so. Or I thought maybe you'd 'hid yourself'. Some people do that, don't they? They hide themselves.

STACEY. It's not really my thing.

ANGELA. I hate when people hide themselves. Like anyone gives a shit.

Silence.

STACEY. I like that dress.

ANGELA. Primark. Fiver.

STACEY. You'd never know. It's lovely.

Beat.

ANGELA. What d'you do then, Stace?

STACEY. Marketing. Third-party promotions. Mostly film clients. Started up my own agency.

ANGELA. Sound.

STACEY. Only tiny. Well, not tiny. There's me and... someone else. A graduate, Claire. She does Mondays, Thursdays and Fridays. I'm thinking of getting someone else for Tuesdays and Wednesdays. Just... really bloody busy. Can't cope.

STACEY laughs nervously again.

No yeah, she's great, Claire. I wouldn't say we're *friends* exactly but we get on.

ANGELA. And why wouldn't you? I hate all that bullshit about women working together. 'How do you cope with all the bitchiness?' You might not be bosom buddies but it doesn't mean you're clawing each other's eyes out over the photocopier, not that we've got a photocopier but d'you know what I mean?

STACEY. God, I know. We get on fine but I socialise with clients, mostly. Not my staff. I think it's a bit tacky.

ANGELA. I go out with the girls in work all the time. We have a right buzz.

STACEY. Yeah, of course, sometimes it's brilliant. Really good for... morale.

ANGELA. Six on the dot, out the door and then I'm just Ang. Not that I'm not Ang at work but there's boundaries, isn't there?

STACEY. What do you do?

ANGELA. Hairdresser. I've got me own shop.

STACEY. Oh, wow, good for you. Well done.

ANGELA. I love it. Every day's different. People sit down in that chair and it's like they're in a confessions box. It all fucking comes out. I don't know where to put meself half the time. It's not just holidays and nights out. I get affairs, STD's... family secrets. They get it *right* off their chest. I should charge extra. They can chunner on all they like. It's all about them, that's the whole point. They want someone to listen to them. And I'm a brilliant listener.

STACEY. You are.

Silence.

ANGELA. Tell us about your job. Your *agency*.

STACEY. Do you eat cereal?

ANGELA. Depends. Which type?

STACEY. Doesn't matter. You know how sometimes there'll be a free toy or a competition on the back of the box?

ANGELA. Oh, aye.

STACEY. That's me. Not *just* cereals, but that's the golden grail. Getting an on-pack.

ANGELA. An 'on-pack'?

STACEY. Yes. Exactly as it sounds really. A promotion that is *on-pack*. (*Beat.*) On the pack. I love it. Work is / I *am* my job.

ANGELA. Are you?

STACEY. Yeah, I mean… No, I'm not / There's other things obviously that… I am, apart from work but… I like my job. (*Beat.*) It's fun.

ANGELA. I entered one of those competitions last year. It was for a holiday.

STACEY. Exactly.

ANGELA. Didn't win obviously.

STACEY. But if you don't enter…

ANGELA. It was to do with this film. They were 'celebrating its release'.

STACEY. There you go. That's how it works. Free advertising for the film company. The cost of the prize is always a fraction of what it would be to pay for coverage on all those cereal boxes so the film company get leverage. I create the partnerships, manage the clients. Seal the deals.

ANGELA. How do you do that then? Seal a deal?

STACEY. Well, it's about liaising with the third-party / So, okay, we're the agency, *I'm* the agency. The client is the film company and the third-party is –

ANGELA. Quaker Oats.

STACEY. In theory, yes. Brilliant. (*Beat.*) It's all about creating synergy though so the film would have to be a good fit –

ANGELA. *Last King of Scotland.*

STACEY. Erm…

ANGELA. Oats. Scotland.

STACEY. Yeah. Okay… Not bad actually.

ANGELA. It's a funny job, innit?

STACEY. I mean, it's a bit more complicated than –

ANGELA. Totally –

STACEY. But that's the general. Thing. There's money to be made, definitely. It's all about contacts. Being creative. Widening the net.

ANGELA. See, that's where I'd fall down, you see. With the contacts. My net is *not* very wide.

STACEY. It just takes time. Seeking out the big brands. Getting direct contact with the heads of marketing. Establishing relationships.

ANGELA. Yeah… I just don't know if I could be arsed.

STACEY. It's a very specific skill.

ANGELA. It's funny cos talking's probably one of me big strengths but it's not talking, is it? It's schmoozing. We had this loyalty night once in the shop, can't even remember what the deal was – book up front for two cut-and-blows and get a colour half price. Something like that. Anyway, I was shit at it. I can talk the legs off a donkey me but every time I went over to someone I felt like I was trying to flog them a timeshare. I worked in a call centre once and I was fine with that. 'Hiya, d'you wanna swap over to BT? No? Right. Fine. Don't blame you. Ta-ra.' Clear-cut. I'm flogging something, I'm not trying to be your mate.

STACEY. Nobody thinks you're trying to be their *friend*.

ANGELA. No. Yeah. Course. (*Beat.*) But right, if I was a cereal person. A marketing director. Is that the top one?

STACEY. In this context, yes.

ANGELA. Good, well, alright. I'd be a bit like… Hang on. (*Beat.*) Ring me. Go on. I'm head of Quaker Oats. Ring me.

STACEY. Oh no... I wouldn't just ring up. Not for an on-pack. I'd email a proposal, and then I'd arrange a time to meet up or call.

ANGELA. Alright. I've got me proposal. Read it all –

STACEY. It's a bit silly.

ANGELA. Oh, just bell me. I'm in the office. (*Beat.*) Go on.

STACEY *reluctantly picks up an imaginary phone and dials a number.* ANGELA *picks up her imaginary phone.*

Good afternoon, Quaker Oats.

STACEY. Hi, could I speak to the marketing director, please?

ANGELA. Speaking.

Beat.

STACEY. Hi, Angela, it's Stacey.

ANGELA. Stacey. Long time. What can I do for you?

STACEY. I was just wondering if you'd had a chance to look through the proposal I sent to you.

ANGELA. Bear with me, Stace... Was this *The Last King of Scotland* one? Yeah, I did, thank you. I've had a *peruse*.

STACEY. Great. I just wanted to get your initial thoughts really.

ANGELA. Okay, well, I've had a mull and I don't think it's for us.

STACEY. Why's that?

ANGELA. For a start, I can't really see the link.

STACEY. Well, it's... Scotland.

ANGELA. Yeah, but the film's about a Ugandan dictator, isn't it? It's not really got anything to do with Scotland.

STACEY. He's Scottish though. The main guy. Not Idi Amin.

ANGELA. Yeah, I see your point.

STACEY. And it's about strength, overcoming... adversity. Quaker Oats give you strength.

ANGELA. Great, great. Yeah. So the prize is a weekend in Edinburgh at a health spa?

STACEY. Yes. And some… merchandise. All we'd want is coverage, in the form of the competition itself, on the back of your boxes.

ANGELA. So it wouldn't cost me a thing?

STACEY. Just the print costs, which –

ANGELA. Whoa, whoa, whoa. How much is that gonna be?

STACEY. I'm not sure. You'd have to get a quote.

ANGELA. Oh, come on, Stace, you've been in this game long enough. Tell it to me straight, you owe me that much.

STACEY. It depends how many units… Oh, I don't know. Two thousand.

ANGELA. Quid?

STACEY. Roughly, yes.

ANGELA. And how much is this weekend costing?

STACEY. I haven't got the figures in front of me –

ANGELA. Because I've done me research and I know for a fact that, all-in, dinner bed and breakfast plus –

STACEY. Sorry but this is a bit stupid. It doesn't work like this. I can't cut hair, I wouldn't even try and this is / There's a lot more to this job… It's a pointless exercise really if you don't understand it. Sorry. I hope you don't think I'm being –

ANGELA. Highly strung. No. Course I don't. *I'm* sorry. I do that when I'm nervous. I'm like a dog with a bone. Sorry.

STACEY. No. God. I'm sorry. It's / Bloody hell, what a silly… So much to talk about, haven't we?

ANGELA. I know. Twenty years.

STACEY. So much to catch up on.

Long pause. ROB *enters puncturing the awkward silence.*
Carrying a shopping bag. He's wet through. ANGELA
chucks the tea towel to him and he dries himself off a bit
before swaggering over to STACEY. *Nonchalant but clearly*
self-conscious.

ROB. Stace.

STACEY *puts her arms around him. They hug awkwardly.*
ROB *pulls away, puts his shopping bags on the floor.*

Shop's fucking miles away.

STACEY. You didn't need to go, we've got plenty here. I
brought tons of food. Loads of booze.

ROB. Well, I didn't know, did I? Didn't expect you to cater for
us. Thought there'd only be enough for three. I got bacon,
sausages –

STACEY. There's plenty of stuff.

ROB. Can't be doing with Quorn, Stace, tofu, any of that shit.

STACEY. I'm not a vegetarian any more.

ROB. Since when?

STACEY. Fifteen years.

Beat. ROB *slips an arm around* ANGELA.

So how did you two… meet?

ROB. Pub.

ANGELA. Romantic. Not.

ROB. I didn't recognise her. I'm just standing there…
mesmerised. Then she comes over and I'm like, I can't
believe this. This *never* happens to me. Not that I'm always
perving over girls. I'm not a perve.

ANGELA. Then I'm like, 'Are you Stacey Walker's brother?'
Proper burst your balloon, didn't I?

ANGELA *laughs.*

(*To* STACEY.) Your ears must have been burning that night.

ROB. Never mind bunking off school, didn't think you even had any mates then. (*To* ANGELA.) Proper geek. Sat in her room all the time. Or I thought she did.

ANGELA. Quiet ones are the worst.

ANGELA *finishes her cigarette. She stubs it out.*

Can I use the loo?

ROB. It's not her house.

ANGELA. It's called *etiquette*.

STACEY. Top of the stairs.

ANGELA *leaves*.

It's... great to see you, Rob.

ROB. Is it?

STACEY. Yes, yeah. Course it is.

ROB. What d'you think then? Me and Angela.

Pause. ROB *picks at the arm of his sweater.*

STACEY. Yeah.

ROB. What does 'yeah' mean?

STACEY. Yeah, I think she's alright. (*Beat.*) She's great. She's absolutely, really... funny and great. I'm very happy for you. That you've met someone.

ROB. No need to sound so surprised.

STACEY. I'm not surprised. Well, I'm surprised, obviously, that you're with *her* –

ROB. *Angela.*

STACEY. Angela. I'm surprised about *that*. I'm not surprised you're with *someone*. A girlfriend. I'm pleased.

Silence.

Do you... like her then?

ROB. Course I like her. Why would I go out with someone I didn't like? Why would I bring her here?

STACEY. I don't know. (*Beat.*) Why would you?

ROB *stares at* STACEY, *confused.*

ROB. You're burning me head out a bit now. She's me girlfriend. I like her. A lot. So I asked her to come. Fucking hell.

STACEY. Okay, sorry. I'm showing an interest, that's all.

ROB. Bit late for that, isn't it?

STACEY. Did you get the money I sent you?

Pause.

ROB. Yeah. Thank you.

STACEY. You're welcome.

ROB. I'll pay you back. (*Reaches into his pocket and pulls out a ten-pound note.*) Here's a tenner for starters.

STACEY. I don't want it back I was just –

ROB. Making a point, putting me down. Trying to make me feel like a –

STACEY. No. Fucking… Christ Almighty.

ROB *puts the note on the side.*

ROB. I'd rather wipe me arse with it. I'd rather wipe my shitty arse with it and flush it down the bog –

STACEY. Stop it.

ROB. You're judgemental, you. You judge people.

STACEY. No I don't.

ROB. Think you're a cut above.

Beat.

STACEY. You're not going to get me to argue with you.

ROB. I'm not trying to get you to argue with me. Just thought you might've been in touch. (*Beat.*) Did you know I was out?

STACEY. I thought you must have been.

ROB. And you had my number.

STACEY. I lost it. (*Beat.*) I'm not going to try and offer any excuses. I didn't come. I apologise about that. I'm sorry.

ROB. Didn't mind you not coming. I *did* mind you *saying* you were coming and then not turning up. I wouldn't even have expected you to come, it was just with you saying and then nothing happening. (*Beat.*) I wouldn't even have thought about it otherwise. Wouldn't even have crossed me mind.

STACEY. I shouldn't have said I'd come and not turn up.

ROB. Felt like a bit of a prick. You tell people you've got a visit and then you sit there and wait and nobody comes. Some of them thought I was lying. Took the piss out of me. What's worse though is the ones who try and be nice because they feel sorry for you. That's fucking darkness, that is. (*Beat.*) She doesn't know, so I'd appreciate –

STACEY. Yes. I gathered as much.

Silence.

How did it… go? (*Beat.*) Inside.

ROB. 'How did it go'? How d'you think it went?

STACEY. Look, I don't know what to / Please stop this. I know you're… upset.

ROB. I'm not upset. I'm happy. Things are good. I'm in a good place. I've been doing lots of work –

STACEY. You're working? Good, that's great. Where?

Beat.

ROB. On meself. Work on meself.

STACEY. Oh. Great. That's really –

ROB. It's important.

STACEY. Course, course. (*Beat.*) Have you actually… Have you got a job though?

ROB. Not yet but I'd prefer it if you didn't –

STACEY. No.

ROB. I'm a chef.

STACEY. Right.

ROB. Not a total blag. Got an interview next week. Some new place in town. Kitchen-hand, chopping veg and all that. It's a start, isn't it?

STACEY. Yeah. That's great.

ROB. Work me way up. Visualisation.

ROB *reaches into his rucksack and pulls out a piece of paper and something else which he hides behind his back. He hands the piece of paper to* STACEY.

STACEY. What's this?

ROB. Certificate. I did a little cookery course inside. And…

ROB *produces a small wooden sculpture from behind his back.*

Happy birthday.

STACEY *takes it and studies it, not quite sure how to respond.*

You've got it upside down.

ROB *takes it off her and turns it the right way.*

It's a bird. I made it.

STACEY. For me?

ROB *nods.* STACEY *is genuinely touched.*

Thank you.

ROB. Took a woodwork class too.

Beat.

STACEY. Mum's going ask you everything about Thailand. Just warning you. Be prepared.

ROB. Sent them postcards.

STACEY. How?

ROB. Some bloke's sister lives there. Cost me a phone card and a packet of Marlborough Light each go. I'd write it, give it him… he'd send it to her in an envelope and then she'd put a stamp on it and post it for me.

STACEY. Very clever.

ROB. He had this big stack from when he went travelling. Some were too nice to send so I used to stick them on me wall. (*Beat.*) I learnt a bit of Thai 'n' all. '*Lot noi dai mai, khorb koon*'… 'Can you make it cheaper, please?' (*Beat.*) '*Sawatdee.*' (*Beat.*) That's 'hello'. (*Beat.*) '*Yet ter.*'

Beat.

STACEY. What's that?

ROB. Look it up.

STACEY *leaves. When she's gone,* ROB *picks up the ten-pound note and puts it back in his pocket.*

THREE

The curtains are closed and the lights are out. MIKE, STACEY *and* ANGELA *sit around the table,* ROB *below everyone on a footstool.* JULIA *enters from the kitchen holding a birthday cake with one large candle in the middle.* JULIA *starts the singing.*

JULIA (*singing*). Happy birthday... C'mon, you miserable lot...

ALL (*singing*). Happy Birthday to you, happy birthday to you, happy birthday, dear Stacey, happy birthday to you.

JULIA *sets the cake down on the table and claps triumphantly.* STACEY *blows the candle out and* JULIA *switches the lights on.* MIKE *opens the bottle of Prosecco on the table and pours it into four flutes.*

STACEY. Oh, you didn't need to do this.

JULIA. Make a wish and don't tell.

MIKE *passes the glasses around. He gets to* ROB *but there's one short.*

We're a flute short.

STACEY. There's glasses in the kitchen.

JULIA. Not flutes though.

ROB. It doesn't matter.

ANGELA. We can share, it's fine.

ROB. Yeah, we can share.

JULIA. It does matter.

STACEY. I'll have a normal glass, you're all guests.

STACEY *goes to stand.* JULIA *stops her.*

JULIA. You will not. Not on your birthday. It's because we thought it was just the four of us.

ANGELA. Sorry, I thought Rob had said –

JULIA. Oh my God, Angela, I didn't mean anything by that. Mike, tell her.

MIKE. Tell her what?

JULIA. We are absolutely… thrilled to have you here. Aren't we?

MIKE. Thrilled.

JULIA. We've heard so much about you, haven't we?

Beat.

MIKE. Yeah.

JULIA. I'll have a normal glass.

ROB. I'll have a normal glass, Mum, it's fine.

MIKE. I'll have a measuring jug if hurries things up a bit.

ROB goes into the kitchen and returns with a mug. He pours the Prosecco into it and holds it up.

ROB. Cheers to Stacey. Happy Birthday.

Everyone follows suit, clinking glasses.

MIKE. To Stacey, happy birthday, sweetheart.

JULIA reaches into her bag and puts a present on the table.

STACEY. Thank you, I feel embarrassed, it's not even my birthday for another –

JULIA (*cuts her off, handing her the present*). This… is a little extra. It's nothing much, just something to keep us near.

STACEY unwraps the gift, it's a framed photograph of the family together, taken years ago when she and ROB were teenagers.

STACEY laughs.

STACEY. Oh my God.

JULIA. Remember?

JULIA *whips the picture out of* STACEY*'s hands and passes it to* ANGELA.

It's us, Angela. Years ago. All together.

MIKE. Watch out, Julia. You'll get cake on it.

JULIA. Stacey's got her brace and Rob's acne's quite bad. We won a competition... Well, we *thought* we'd won a competition the way they sold it to us. Richard from next-door-but-one put our names down, which was nice of him. We went to a proper photography studio and everything. They sent us a couple of these little miniatures afterwards and there's the catch you see... if you wanted a life-size one –

MIKE. They weren't *life*-size.

JULIA. Okay, bigger... If you wanted one of the big ones then you had to pay full price and we're not talking coppers either... They were about, what? Two... three hundred pound, Mike?

MIKE. Three hundred and twenty-five plus VAT.

JULIA. Bloody rip-off. We offered them a price, didn't we? We said... max, what was it, Mike? Hundred? Hundred and fifty?

MIKE. One seven five.

JULIA. But they said that it wasn't something we could barter over and that we should have read the small print. We wrote to *Watchdog*, didn't we? Never heard anything but anyway they didn't ask for this back so I kept it. (*Beat.*) I like it this small anyway. I can carry us all round with me. (*Beat.*) Richard bought two, didn't he? Of the life-size ones.

MIKE. They're not life-size.

JULIA. He's got one in his front living room.

MIKE. You've never even been into Richard's.

JULIA. You can see it through the window. Lovely big gilt frame. They get away with it because the wallpaper's so plain. Cream background with ever such a faint design in a slightly darker shade… Biscuit, you'd say it was. Or mushroom. Anyway, it's very tasteful. Probably Laura Ashley. I look in every time I'm going to the PDSA.

MIKE. Julia does a hell of a lot for charity, Angela, but she'll never tell you. Very big on animals. Can't open the paper without getting upset when one of those pamphlets falls out.

ANGELA. I'm the same. Grew up with rescue dogs. Makes you shudder to think what they've been through. One of them, Lady, she was fine with women, girls, but if a bloke went near her she shook like a leaf, ears went right back. Sometimes she got diarrhoea. They're just like humans, aren't they, dogs, when it comes to nerves?

JULIA. Oh, don't. I couldn't sleep the other night. I was in town, shopping in the afternoon and there was one of those stands… these animal-welfare people. They had this photo of a dog. A schnauzer I think he was. Bubbles. Lovely looking little thing. Anyway, they'd rescued him from these people in a council block. He had spent every day of his little life, up until that moment, with all his legs tied together being dragged around the flat by the kids. They stuffed him in a pair of women's tights once and lowered him out of the window into a wheelie bin. There were before-and-after snaps. You couldn't recognise him as the same dog. I have nightmares about it. (*Beat.*) Some people shouldn't be allowed pets.

MIKE. Scum.

JULIA. They should sterilise them. (*Beat.*) It's not that I won't talk about it. I will talk about it but only if it's appropriate. I'm not one for blowing my own trumpet.

ANGELA. But you do yer bit. Gotta do your bit, haven't yer?

JULIA. Exactly.

MIKE. She does do her bit.

JULIA. There's a charity shop by ours, especially for cats with AIDS. Breaks my heart every time I go past. I didn't even know cats could get it, but they can. Cat AIDS they call it.

MIKE. It's drugs, isn't it? Most of the time.

JULIA. No, they get it through fighting apparently. It's passed on through their little bite wounds.

MIKE. Not the fucking cats, Julia. The people. High as kites. Off their bloody heads on Christ knows what. Sniffing glue and sucking on ecstasy.

ROB *smirks*.

There's nothing funny about drugs. Or the scumbags who sell them. All on that estate... You know somewhere's the arse-end of the earth when you see adults riding around on children's bikes. Only just got the car back. Some bastard scratched the side of it. Old Merc. Nothing fancy. 300SL.

JULIA. I've been trying to think of anyone with a grudge.

MIKE. Kids, isn't it? Little bastards.

JULIA. Some of them on that Brookvale Estate. Animals.

STACEY (*trying to shush* JULIA). Mum.

JULIA. Tuesday it was and one rides right in front of me on his bike. Does one of those... wheelies. Trying to frighten me. I said, 'You'll have to try harder than that, you little...' Should have heard what came out of his mouth. Absolutely disgusting... 'You mother-effing this... You 'C'-sucking that.' Mike nearly went out with an umbrella but I stopped him. I said, 'You know what'll happen... You'll only end up getting in trouble yourself.' I had to go back home and have a sweet tea. I never have sugar tea these days. It's strictly herbal. Darjeeling usually. But I was so upset.

MIKE. Where are you from, Angela?

ANGELA. The Brookvale Estate.

JULIA. Aww.

ANGELA. I live in Leesdale Road now though.

MIKE. Good for you.

JULIA. And you're doing well, aren't you, Robbie love? How's the job?

ROB. Alright. Yeah.

JULIA. 'Alright'… Angela, is he like this with you? I bet he's not like this with you, is he? It's like he's a kid all over again. 'How was school, Rob?' 'Alright'… D'you know, once he comes home, drops his bags, stomps into the kitchen and I ask him, same as always, 'How was school?' and course it was 'alright'. Next day I get a phone call from the headmaster. 'Is Robert out of hospital yet?' The little B.

MIKE. Very different heads on them, these two, Angela. Same start. Same opportunities. Same things we sacrificed, wasn't it, Julia?

JULIA. I don't think of them as sacrifices. You don't, do you? When it's for your kids. And most people don't even get one holiday a year, do they?

MIKE. More than a bloody holiday a year. That school. And what did you get, Rob? In your exams.

ROB. You should know. 'Sall you go on about.

MIKE. Can't bring meself to say it. Might choke.

ROB. A 'D' in PE.

MIKE. A 'D' in PE. That's it. (*Beat.*) That. Is. It. Give him a penny for his thoughts, you'd get change.

ANGELA. 'Snot bad. You could do a BTEC with that. Go on to teacher-training.

MIKE. He's nearly forty.

ROB. Got a job anyway. I like me job.

MIKE (*hasn't heard*). A 'D' in PE. He couldn't even get a decent grade for kicking a fucking ball round a muddy field. There was a lad in his class, Angela, wore calipers. He got a 'C'.

ROB. He did rowing.

ANGELA. You could do rowing at your school?

MIKE. Oh, Christ, you could do indoor skiing if you wanted. Fantastic facilities.

ROB. You couldn't do skiing.

MIKE. Yes, you could.

ROB. They had a day trip to a dry slope. Once. That was it.

MIKE. What's your point?

ROB. Well, that's not being able to 'do skiing'. You're making it sound like –

MIKE. I tell you what bloody beggars belief now, Angela. The fact that he's a *cook*. God only knows how. (*Beat.*) Parents' night, one time. We bowl up. Not expecting the best but, you know… hopeful. Gets in there. First up's Home Economics. I mean, it makes me bloody laugh that he's chosen that for an option but, you know, if he likes it.

ANGELA. It's the things you enjoy that you're best at.

MIKE. Exactly. And he'd brought some scones home the week before that weren't half bad so, y'know, as I say. Hopeful. (*Beat.*) So we sit down in front of this woman. Pinched face, quite highly strung… What was her name now?

ROB. Mrs Taylor. If you're gonna tell it can you just get on with it?

MIKE. Starts off bad enough. Short attention span, clumsy, won't stop talking, then she gets to his end-of-year project –

ROB. It was a practical, it wasn't a project.

MIKE. Whatever. She made them all cook something. A meal. You could pick whatever you wanted, bring in the ingredients, make it and then she marks it.

ANGELA. Bit like *MasterChef*.

MIKE. Well… anyway, guess what soft-lad makes?

ANGELA. Scones?

MIKE. Fucking Pot Noodle.

ANGELA. I like Pot Noodles.

MIKE. I like crisps but I wouldn't open a bag of Wotsits and expect to get a fucking O-Level for it.

ROB. I did it on purpose. She was a fascist.

MIKE. Oh, well then. That told her, didn't it. (*Beat*.) Mind you, at least that was something, Christ knows what he did with the others.

ROB. Maths, I got stoned on the back field. Chemistry, back field. English, can't remember. Physics, went to the girls' school and got off with Stephanie Barwise.

ANGELA. I know Stephanie Barwise. She went out with me cousin for a bit. Long gums and tiny teeth.

ROB. They reckoned I would've done alright 'n' all. Predicted mostly 'C's. Just couldn't be arsed.

ROB *and* MIKE *eye each other*.

ANGELA. Goes to show you though, doesn't it? Exams, they're not the be-all and end-all.

JULIA. What do you do again, Ang?

ANGELA. Hairdresser.

JULIA *covers her head with her hands*.

JULIA. Oh, what must you think of me? What a state. Are you mobile?

ANGELA. No. Curl Up and Dye in the Conny.

ROB. She owns it.

MIKE. Good for you.

JULIA. Curl Up and Dye? By the main entrance just as you come in? I walk past most days. I probably see you. Snipping away inside. (*Beat*.) It's for younger women, isn't it? Highlights, funny fringes… that sort of thing.

ANGELA. We do all sorts. I could give you a discount.

JULIA. You wouldn't want me coming in. Spoiling your reputation. I'd put people off, wouldn't I? In my rollers. Anyway, I have a woman comes round. Every Thursday. But thank you, that is very very kind.

ANGELA. Stick your head in next time. Say hello.

JULIA. Well, this is it. I could call past when I'm going to the cat AIDS place. I go about once a month then usually I'll have a spot of lunch somewhere afterwards. I went to your old place last week, Stace. What's it called? Oh, God, little café... very brightly decorated. You'd think it was run by ethnics but it's that white woman with the nose ring. Stacey had a Saturday job there –

STACEY. Chapter.

JULIA. Chapter, that's it. She's still there, Stace. I told her what you were up to. She was very impressed. You liked it there, didn't you?

STACEY. It was alright. For a Saturday job. Cathleen was nice.

JULIA. *Cathleen.* Let you put your little paintings up on the wall, didn't she? She's everso good at drawing, aren't you, Stace?

STACEY. Not any more.

JULIA. Some of the ones you used to bring home from school. Hand on heart, you would not have told the difference between them and something you might see hanging in a gallery. (*Beat.*) I wish I'd kept them now. I've got a phobia about clutter, Angela. Why didn't you keep it up, Stace?

STACEY. I dunno really, I suppose –

MIKE. Because she had a bit of bloody ambition about her.

JULIA. Do you ever go in there for your lunch, Ang? Chapter?

ANGELA. I take butties in.

JULIA. You're like me. I never have sandwiches out. You don't know who's had their fingers on them, do you? They're not really that big on sarnies in Chapter anyway though, are they, Stace?

MIKE. All couscous and people in wheelchairs.

JULIA. There *was* a few wheelchairs in there. I thought maybe they were having some sort of day out.

ROB. Angela's dad was in a wheelchair.

JULIA. Aww. Why is he in a wheelchair, Angela?

ANGELA. Well, he's not now –

JULIA. Oh, lovely –

ANGELA. – he's dead.

JULIA. Oh, Christ. I'm sorry. (*Beat.*) Robbie didn't mention it. Robbie, why didn't you mention about Angela's dad?

ANGELA. It was ages ago.

JULIA. Was he in poor health?

MIKE. He died, Julia.

JULIA. We're with Bupa and you're entitled to a free health check with our package.

MIKE. Gold. We would have gone platinum but I think this one covers all the bases, doesn't it? I go once a month.

JULIA. I just go when they send me a letter. I don't want to be a nuisance.

MIKE. We're paying out good money, Julia.

JULIA. Why was your dad in the wheelchair, Angela?

ANGELA. He lost his legs in an accident.

JULIA. Awww. (*To* MIKE.) Your Uncle Mike didn't have any legs, did he?

MIKE. He had one.

JULIA. One then. Oh, he loves to split hairs, Angela. (*Beat.*) Was that how he died? Because of the accident?

STACEY. Mum, leave it alone now, eh?

ANGELA. He was a big smoker. Sixty a day.

JULIA. Aww. (*To* MIKE.) I forced you to give up, didn't I?

MIKE. You didn't force me.

JULIA. I said, 'I'm not going to be a widow at sixty just because of your selfish stupid bloody habit.' I don't know how people afford it anyway, at least it was just the health issue with us, but you see them, don't you? Puffing away outside the Job Centre.

MIKE. Idiots. Richard did hypnotherapy. He's never looked back.

MIKE *reaches in his pocket and pulls out a fat cigar. He holds it up.*

My little treat though, Cohiba Robustos. Cuban. Fifty quid a pop. The way I look at it, you can treat yourself once a fortnight or puff away every night on a cheap Hamlet. I'm quality over quantity every time.

ANGELA. Long as you're enjoying yourself, Mike. That's what life's all about, innit?

MIKE. Exactly. Work hard all your life. Do things by the book. If you can't reap the benefits now.

MIKE *puffs on the cigar. He nods.*

ANGELA. What was it you did?

MIKE. Management consultancy. Very rewarding. On the whole. Not without its ups and downs… like most things in life.

ANGELA. Management consultancy. What's that exactly? Sorry, does that make me –

MIKE. No, not at all. (*Takes a huge puff of his cigar.*) Broadly speaking, it's helping organisations improve their performance, primarily through the analysis of existing business problems. 'The successful man is the one who finds out what's wrong with his business before his competitors do.' We're quite big in chemicals. You don't actually need to know a hell of a lot about the products but I like to think I've got a pretty comprehensive grasp on the industry.

Silence.

The key to success is this: clients don't want to hear about what they're doing wrong, so you have to wax lyrical about their strengths then slip the criticism in when they're not looking. It's like feeding vegetables to kids.

ANGELA. Money in it?

MIKE. Yes. Yeah... enough. But then we'd all like more money, wouldn't we? (*Beat.*) My dad was a docker. We grew up nine of us in a two-bed house. Slept on the floor, pissed in a bedpan, shat outside in a bucket. If that doesn't give you motivation, nothing will.

ANGELA. Do you work, Julia?

MIKE (*snorting*). You're joking, aren't you? (*Beat.*) Yes, actually, I beg your pardon... she has got a job. Full-time shopper. Insatiable appetite for shoes and curtains.

JULIA. Oh, shut up, Mike. Now, come on, Robbie... we want to hear all about it. *Thailand.*

MIKE. Beautiful country, Thailand. People are very friendly. Humble.

ROB. How would you know?

JULIA. Was it awfully hot, Robbie? Richard's daughter lives in Australia. They celebrate Christmas in August, isn't that funny? Anyway. We're not talking about Australia, are we? We're talking about Thailand. Go on, Robbie.

ROB. It was life-changing.

MIKE. How can sitting on your backside on a beach all day swigging lager be life-changing?

ROB. I didn't sit on me arse. Apart from when I meditated. It's a really spiritual place.

MIKE. Oh, Christ.

ROB. I did a yoga retreat.

JULIA. I'd love to do yoga but I'm terrified of breaking wind. I don't think I'd ever get over it. Do you do yoga in London, Stacey?

STACEY. Ashtanga.

ROB. I met a guru –

JULIA. Do you do yoga, Angela?

ROB *sinks back into his chair, takes a swig of his drink.*

ANGELA. Zumba.

JULIA. Now I've heard about this Zumba. Is it for young ones?

MIKE (*puffing on his cigar, enjoying* ROB's *frustration*). Robert is trying to tell a story, Julia.

JULIA. I'm sorry, love, go on.

ROB. Can't remember what I was saying.

STACEY. You met a guru in Thailand.

JULIA. A guru? Did you?

ROB. He could breathe through his eyes.

Silence. ANGELA *snorts with laughter,* STACEY *follows.*

JULIA. Through his eyes? What's the point in that?

MIKE. Well, it's helpful if you're bunged up, isn't it?

ROB. He'd reached a higher level of consciousness.

MIKE. Reached for a bloody crack pipe, more like.

ROB. 'In order to experience everyday spirituality we need to remember that we are spiritual beings spending time in a human body.'

MIKE. Life's a bitch and then you die. Sorry if you're religious, Angela.

ANGELA. Atheist.

MIKE. Sensible girl. Head on your shoulders. Load of bloody bullshit.

JULIA. I don't know what you'd call me. (*Raises her hand towards* MIKE.) Don't, Mike, whatever it is you're going to say, nobody's interested in your silly jokes.

STACEY. Agnostic.

JULIA. What?

STACEY. I think you're agnostic. You're undecided.

ROB. No.

STACEY. What d'you mean 'no'?

ROB. Agnosticism is neither believing nor disbelieving.

STACEY. Undecided.

ROB. Undecided implies that you're gonna make a decision. An agnostic just accepts they don't know. There's a difference.

STACEY. No there *isn't* –

JULIA. Well, all I know is that I had an experience once. No idea what you'd call it, but it was definitely something from another plane, if you get me. It was when I had my veins done. They put me out, the way they do. I don't know if you've ever been put out, Angela, but they say this thing. They go, 'Try and count to ten,' and you know you won't be able to and they know you know you won't be able to. I think it's meant to be like a sort of comfort but personally I find it bloody terrifying. Anyway I got to, I don't know, six or something and I'm out cold. But then I have these… I want to say visions. I can't really describe it properly but there's all beautiful colours and I'm a lot younger. Mike isn't around. It's like he doesn't exist. I remember feeling really really happy, really light, do you know what I mean? Carefree. Then the next minute, the bloke who works in the Co-op on Heath Road. The little Indian man. What's he called, Mike?

MIKE. How the bloody hell would I know?

ANGELA. Shiv. He delivers the magazines for the salon.

JULIA. He's a nice little chap, isn't he? He's not even particularly little. I don't know why we call him that. Anyway, he's there and he's holding his hand out to me. It's like he's floating almost, peddling the air, and I'm just about to take his hand when they wake me up and it's all over.

STACEY. So basically, you had a dream.

JULIA. Not a dream as we know it. It was like some sort of near-death experience.

MIKE. A near-death experience usually involves nearly dying, Julia.

JULIA. Who's to say I didn't? All I know is something happened to me on that operating table. Something out of this world.

STACEY. What's the significance of the man from the Co-op then?

JULIA. I don't know. That's all part of the mystery, isn't it?

ROB. It's the butterfly effect. People you barely even know can change the course of your life every day without you even realising.

MIKE. Here we go, hold on to your hats.

ROB. You're walking down the street, yeah? And someone's walking towards you so you step to the other side, then *because* you move out the way, you might, I dunno –

ANGELA. Step in dogshit.

Beat.

ROB. Alright, okay… Step in shit. And you stop to wipe the shit off.

JULIA. It's disgusting how many people let their dogs do that, isn't it? Some girl the other day on her phone, chatting away and the bloody dog's crouched in front of her, straining. I always took a sandwich bag and a surgical glove out for Norman, didn't I? They used to give me a load when I popped into the doctors. That's how they knew he'd died actually. They were everso lovely about it. Barbara, it was, the older one, she said, 'I hope you don't mind me asking, Mrs Walker, but it's been such a long time since you've asked for any gloves, is it bad news?' (*Beat.*) It's amazing really, how you think you're over something then all it takes is someone to make a little comment like that and you're in bloody bits. I'm sorry, Rob, finish your story.

MIKE. You stood in dogshit.

ROB. It was hypothetical.

MIKE. You stood in a hypothetical dogshit.

Beat.

ROB. And... because you've stopped, you don't get hit by a bus that you would've got hit by two minutes before if that person hadn't made you step to the other side of the pavement.

MIKE. How profound. (*Beat.*) What other pearls of wisdom did they teach you in spirit school then?

ROB. Spirit*ual.* And it wasn't *school.* It was a *retreat.*

JULIA. What you're saying is then, Rob, that the little man from the Co-op could have saved my life?

ROB. You don't know, do you? He might have kept you chatting that bit longer one day. And that stopped something from happening or he might just have inspired you to do one small thing that led to another bigger thing. It's not all about life and death.

JULIA. I don't know about inspiring me, I can't even understand what he says half the time.

MIKE. Believe what you like if it makes you happy. I wanna enjoy life, not hang all me hopes on some make-believe paradise. And even if there was a Heaven, I've worked hard all me life. Got meself a decent pension. What bloody use is it up there?

ROB. Think you're a bit wide of the point there.

MIKE. There *is* no flaming point. That's what I'm on about.

ROB. What about fulfilment?

MIKE. I'm very fulfilled, me, matey. I'm not one of these idiots who retires then has a bloody heart attack because they don't know what to do with themselves. You get up, do things, keep yourself young, it's all in the head.

JULIA. Was it all-inclusive, Rob?

ROB. Nah, didn't even get a hotel some nights. Slept on the beach. Under the stars.

JULIA. What if it rained?

ROB. It's Thailand, Mum. Doesn't fuckin' rain in Thailand, does it?

STACEY. Apart from monsoon season.

ROB. It didn't rain when I was there. The weather was perfect.

ANGELA. Aww, I'd love to go to Thailand.

MIKE. You're not very brown.

ROB. I've been back ages.

JULIA. He doesn't tan easy. He's got that sort of complexion. Used to go through buckets of factor with him as a kid, Angela. Were you sensible, Rob? He needs fifty really. Did you use fifty?

ROB. Yeah, Mum. (*Beat*.) Hardly sunbathed anyway. Too much goin' on, too much to see –

JULIA. You can still burn. Just being out in it. Even when it's cloudy.

ROB. Went diving every day. Best feeling in the world. Get such a buzz. It's like being on another planet... Fish out of cartoons swimming right in front of your face. You can eat like a king on a quid a day. And the sunsets. You've never even *seen* a sunset unless you've been to Thailand.

MIKE. I very seldom burn.

JULIA. You've got a lovely colour, Angela.

ANGELA. Spray-on.

JULIA. No? It looks so natural.

ANGELA. St Tropez it in the salon. Come in, I'll do you.

ROB *reaches in his pocket and pulls out a small pile of tatty photos.*

ROB. I've got photos.

JULIA (*to* ANGELA). Do you go… all over?

ANGELA *nods.*

ANGELA. You get paper knickers, like.

JULIA (*laughing*). Oooh.

ANGELA. Friday afternoons we do a free glass of bubbly afterwards.

JULIA. I think I'd bloody need it *before*. Pardon my French.

JULIA *laughs, slightly hyper.*

STACEY. Rob's got photographs.

JULIA. What of, Rob?

Beat.

ROB. Thailand.

JULIA. Ooh, how exciting, let's have a look.

ROB *passes the photographs to* JULIA, *she passes them round.*

(*Flicking through them.*) Oh, lovely. Doesn't it look lovely, Stace?

STACEY. Paradise.

ROB. They don't do it justice.

MIKE *glances at them.*

MIKE. Aren't there any of you?

ROB. Nobody to take them, was there? On me own.

STACEY. Should have asked someone.

ROB. It wasn't Marbella.

MIKE. I don't go to Marbella.

ROB. Whatever. It wasn't your usual commercial wank-trap –

JULIA. Jesus. Robert. 'Scuse me, Angela.

STACEY. Only about fifty million tourists a year. What is a 'wank-trap' anyway?'

JULIA. Will you stop it, the pair of you –

ROB. People holding fucking… pineapples with straws in them. Grinning like whoppers –

STACEY. Having a nice time –

ROB. Delusional.

STACEY *stares at* ROB *in disbelief. He avoids her glare and continues with the photos, handing them around.*

ANGELA (*about the photo*). He climbed to the top of that, Julia.

JULIA. You never did?

ROB *nods, slightly losing confidence in his fantasy.*

He's got a real spirit of adventure, haven't you, Robbie?

MIKE. Phone call once in a while wouldn't have gone amiss.

JULIA. It's expensive, Mike.

MIKE. Email's free.

ROB. Don't know your email address.

MIKE. You would if you'd bothered to ring.

JULIA. Do they have phones there though, Robbie?

MIKE. Course they have bloody phones. It's not Mars. (*Beat.*) Postcard even. Let us know you're not dead.

ROB. I sent postcards.

MIKE. No you didn't.

JULIA. It doesn't matter, does it? You're back now.

ROB. It does matter cos I sent them. I sent about ten.

JULIA. They must have got lost in the post.

MIKE. All ten of them.

JULIA. I expect their postal system isn't very up to date.

MIKE. Prehistoric by the sounds of it.

JULIA. Now, come on… we don't want to argue in front of
    Angela.

MIKE. Who's arguing? I'm not arguing. (*Beat*.) Just can't be
    doing with liars.

ROB. I sent you ten postcards.

Silence.

STACEY. Who wants another drink?

JULIA. I will, Stace. Same again. I'd have a gin but I can't mix
    my drinks. I get in the party spirit and I get a bit excited and
    if someone's offering something, I think… Oh, go on then.
    But then that's it. Cart on its side, apples everywhere.

ANGELA (*holding up her glass*). I'm okay with this, thanks.

    STACEY *stands and starts preparing the drinks.*

MIKE. Try a wine, I've brought some beauties there.

ROB. She doesn't like wine.

JULIA. Stacey drinks *Prosecco*. I'd never even heard of
    Prosecco till we went to London.

MIKE. I bet if you started off with something nice and mellow,
    Angela, you'd be alright. You just haven't developed the
    taste. I did a course. Just a short one but it was quite intense.
    Learnt about the different regions and the grapes. Sort of like
    an overview. I tend to be quite picky now when it comes to
    my wine.

JULIA. I got it for him for Christmas a couple of years ago off the internet. Red Letter Days dot com. We had a day at a vineyard, didn't we? We were a bit disappointed because we were told we'd get an evening meal but it was more like a cheese board really.

MIKE. They had ham as well.

JULIA. You want something hot when you're paying out that much, don't you?

MIKE *swishes the wine around his mouth and swallows*.

MIKE. Not bad. Not bad at all.

JULIA. It's a nice thing to do though. Maybe we could all go. The six of us.

MIKE. I don't know about that. Rob at a wine-tasting. Doesn't know his arse from a hole in the ground when it comes to things like this, I hardly think he's likely to appreciate the difference between a Merlot and a Shiraz.

ANGELA. What is the difference?

Pause.

MIKE. Shiraz is much more…

ROB. Much more what?

MIKE. Give me a minute. I'm trying to put it into less *specialist* terminology.

JULIA. They do have some funny descriptions at these things. Why you'd be in the slightest bit inclined to drink something that tastes like leather –

MIKE. Spicier. Bit more oaky.

JULIA. 'Oaky.' It's crazy.

MIKE. Merlot's lighter… less acidic.

ANGELA. I think he's just reading the label, Julia.

JULIA *shrieks with laughter*.

MIKE. I didn't read the label.

ANGELA. I was only joking.

ROB. He doesn't do jokes.

JULIA. He couldn't take a joke if they were handing them out free in Tescos.

   MIKE *ignores* JULIA. *He leaves to go and get the wine.*

ANGELA. I've always drunk vodka. Since I was kid. Well, teenager, y'know.

JULIA. They start everso early these days. I see them from the estate with their bottles of whatever it is. They look about twelve, some of them.

ANGELA. Me dad drunk quite a bit –

JULIA. Well, who could blame him?

ANGELA. Put me off really. Never gone mad for it. Reckon that's why me and Stace hit it off. We weren't into all that when we were teenagers, were we? Standing on street corners drinking Thunderbirds.

   Beat.

STACEY. No.

ANGELA. Not all estate kids are like that. I wasn't, was I, Stace?

STACEY. No.

ANGELA. We hardly ever even went out anyway at night, did our routines in me bedroom, didn't we?

JULIA. Have I missed something?

STACEY. We were pals, me and Angela. Years ago. For a bit.

JULIA. Oh, Angela, I feel terrible. Did we meet you? Did you come round to the house and I've forgotten? Stacey, did you bring Angela round and I forgot?

   STACEY *is flustered, she starts clearing plates from the table.*

ANGELA. You wouldn't have recognised me. I was quite hefty in those days. Puppy fat. Looked a bit like a lad. (*Beat*.) She might've been embarrassed of me.

STACEY. I wasn't embarrassed. What a thing / Course I wasn't… embarrassed.

JULIA. She was terrible as a teenager, Ang. *Everything* embarrassed her.

STACEY. I wasn't embarrassed of you.

JULIA. We'd be out shopping and some girl from school would see her and shout, give a little wave… Well, you'd think she'd just been flashed. (*Beat*.) Beetroot.

STACEY. I was getting bullied.

JULIA. Girls can be terribly catty, can't they, at that age? I think they were jealous mostly. (*Beat*.) Do you want kids, Angela?

ROB. Mum –

JULIA. I mean in general, as a woman. Not necessarily with you.

ANGELA. Yeah, I do. Definitely.

STACEY. I thought you hated kids.

ANGELA. No.

STACEY. You always used to say –

ANGELA. When I was fourteen. Didn't want them then, did I?

Beat.

STACEY. I know, I just remember –

JULIA. You see them though, don't you? Pushing buggies. Not a jot of embarrassment. There was a girl in the Conny last week, she had one on top and one underneath like a bag of spuds. Can't have been older than seventeen.

ROB. I want kids. Definitely.

Beat.

JULIA. Aww, he'd make a brilliant dad.

  MIKE *enters, clutching a bottle of wine.*

  We're talking about kids, Mike. That business in school with those girls picking on Stacey.

STACEY. More than picking –

  MIKE *holds up the wine proudly.*

MIKE. Châteauneuf du Pape, 1993. Forty quid a bottle. Get the corkscrew, Julia. (*Beat.*) Give the cat the bloody goldfish.

FOUR

MIKE *stands in the centre of the room, arms folded, everyone sits looking at him.* JULIA *in the armchair and* STACEY *next to* ANGELA *on the couch.*

ROB *sits on the floor.* MIKE *clears his throat and makes a 'book' gesture.*

JULIA. Book.

  MIKE *taps his nose, then holds two fingers up.*

  Two words.

  MIKE *taps his nose. Holds one finger up.*

  First word.

  MIKE *taps his nose.*

  You don't need to tap your nose every time.

MIKE. How do you know you've got it right if I don't tap my nose?

JULIA. Well, if you just carry on then I'll presume I'm right.

MIKE. What if you're not right?

JULIA. If I'm not right then you should have a gesture but if I am then you should just carry on.

MIKE. If you're not right I'll do this. (*Waggles his finger.*)

JULIA. Yes, do that.

MIKE. Okay, where were we?

JULIA. A book. Two words. First word.

MIKE *holds one finger up.*

Yes, first word, we know that.

MIKE *spreads his arms out wide.*

Arms.

MIKE *waggles his finger. He does the gesture again, circling the air with his hands.*

Round.

MIKE *waggles his finger.*

Big.

MIKE *puts one finger on his nose and points at* JULIA.

Big? First word big.

MIKE *waggles his finger.*

It's not big? You can't touch your nose and point, Mike, if it's not right.

MIKE *is getting agitated, he waves his arms and then waggles his ear gesturing 'sounds like'.*

Sounds like big... pig, fig, jig, dig, wig.

MIKE *waves his arms around, waggling his finger furiously before shaking his hand from side to side.*

What? I don't know what that means... Does anyone know what that means?

ROB. 'Similar' not 'sounds like'.

MIKE *touches his nose and points to* ROB *enthusiastically.*

JULIA. Similar to big not sounds like? Well, you shouldn't do sounds like if it's not that… Erm, let me think… Similar to big, similar to big…

MIKE *indicates 'sounds like' again and mimes picking up a sandwich and eating it, he wipes his mouth dramatically.*

Sounds like sandwich?

MIKE *waggles his finger.*

Eating…

MIKE *indicates 'nearly' (past tense).*

Eat… ate. Ate.

MIKE *touches his nose and points.*

Sounds like ate, sounds like ate… sounds like ate.

ROB. *Great Expectations.*

MIKE *touches his nose and points.*

JULIA. Oh, Robbie, well done. That is… How did you guess that so quickly?

MIKE. Your turn, Rob.

ROB. I don't want to.

JULIA. Come on, Robbie, don't be a spoilsport.

ROB. I don't want to.

MIKE. Julia, you have a go.

JULIA. It's not my turn.

MIKE. That doesn't necessarily matter.

JULIA *gets up and stands awkwardly in the middle of the room. She thinks, gestures that it's a film.*

Film.

JULIA *taps her nose and points.*

ROB. *Jaws.*

JULIA *taps her nose and points, shrieking with delight.*

MIKE. I don't think it's in line with the spirit of the game. We all knew it was *Jaws*. The generous thing would be to indulge your mother. (*Beat.*) Angela?

ANGELA. I'm alright, thanks.

JULIA. Don't worry about jumping the queue.

ANGELA. I'm not very good at playing games. I forget all the rules.

JULIA. This is what it was like in our day, Ang. Wasn't it, Mike? We didn't have the money to go gallivanting like they do these days. We stayed in and made our own fun.

JULIA *shrieks with laughter.*

Oh my God, that sounds terrible. I didn't mean it like it that. There was none of that was there, Mike?

MIKE. No. There wasn't.

JULIA. No, it was all very traditional. Silly really. I mean, I'm not saying I'm in favour of promiscuity but you wouldn't buy a car without taking it for a test-drive first, would you?

MIKE. Julia.

JULIA. What? You said it, Mike, it's you who bloody said it. And d'you know what? I think you're right. I think I might have reconsidered if I'd had a dabble off the forecourt first.

STACEY. Okay, that's enough now, thank you. I don't think anybody wants to hear about your dabbling.

JULIA. I didn't dabble, that's what I'm saying, things were very different then.

STACEY. We know things were different then, you don't have to go on about it.

JULIA. She's always been like this, Angela. Prudish.

STACEY. I'm not prudish.

JULIA. Takes after my mother.

STACEY. I never even met your mother.

JULIA. It's in the genes.

STACEY. There's a difference between being prudish and not wanting to talk about sex in front of your parents.

ANGELA. None of us would be here if it weren't for sex. Gotta have an open mind about these things.

JULIA. Course you have. It's only natural, in the appropriate circumstances.

ANGELA. Had to in our house. Me mum and dad were at it hammer and tongs. Couldn't get away from it. Walls like tissue paper.

Silence.

JULIA. And he was okay, was he, Angela? With his legs.

ANGELA. Certainly sounded like it.

JULIA. Aww. (*Beat.*) Did he have any help? Like any sort of apparatus?

MIKE. Okay, Julia, Jesus. Talk about crossing lines. You need bloody binoculars to see how far you've gone sometimes.

JULIA. Oh, listen to it. You have to bear with him, Angela. Since he's been retired –

MIKE. I'm not retired, as it happens. I was retired. But now I'm not. (*Beat.*) I'm coming out. Of retirement.

JULIA. Since when?

MIKE. Since I shook hands with my new client.

JULIA. What new client?

MIKE. She's sitting right in front of you.

JULIA. Angela.

MIKE. No, not bloody Angela. Stacey.

STACEY. We haven't really talked about it yet properly.

MIKE. What's there to talk about?

STACEY. I want to make sure you're... happy.

MIKE. I'm happy, forget about it.

JULIA. Stacey's your client?

STACEY. It's not really like I'm Dad's client. It just made...
sense. An opportunity came up.

MIKE. Life in the old dog yet.

ANGELA. What's the opportunity?

MIKE. Stacey's looking to expand, aren't you?

STACEY. Yeah, sort of –

MIKE. And that's where I come in.

STACEY. A one-off sort of... project.

MIKE. Like a sort of partner.

STACEY. Like a sort of silent partner.

MIKE. Not exactly silent.

STACEY. No, not silent. Not totally.

JULIA. What is a *silent* partner? I've always wondered that.

ROB. Money-man.

STACEY. It's not about the money.

MIKE. It's about the expertise.

STACEY. Exactly. It's about Dad's... expertise.

MIKE. If you had a business, Rob.

ROB. I don't wanna business.

ANGELA. You might have one, one day. You might have your
own restaurant.

MIKE *snorts. He ducks an imaginary object.*

MIKE. Watch out, low-flying pig. (*Beat.*) Hey, Stace, tell Rob and Angela about what happened with David last Christmas.

STACEY. Oh… no –

MIKE. Come on. It's only us.

STACEY. No, I don't… It sounds –

ANGELA. Oh, go on.

Pause.

STACEY. His boss –

MIKE. Clive.

STACEY. Clive, called him into his office one day a few weeks before Christmas –

MIKE. He's straight down the line, this fella, straight to the point –

STACEY. He called David into his office a few weeks before Christmas. Said he needed to talk to him –

MIKE. Can you imagine that? Poor bloody fella. Heart must've been in his mouth.

STACEY. And he gives him this big speech about how difficult it's been this year and how it's affecting people's bonuses –

MIKE. Cracked me up, that. D'you know what I imagine when you tell this story, Stace? I imagine Clive with one of those indoor-golf things, d'you know what I mean? You always see them on films and stuff. Luke Taylor had one in our place. Pompous, self-righteous little shit. Anyway, David's sitting there, sweating like an Arab in customs… Go on, Stace.

STACEY. Then he, Clive… apologises to David and he says he knows that this probably isn't what he's expecting –

MIKE *throws his head back and laughs loudly.*

– and he reaches into his desk drawer, gets a box of chocolates out and hands them to David.

MIKE (*shaking his head*). Box of Quality Street.

STACEY (*hurriedly, cringing*). And then he tells / Says to David to open it and he did and there was just… there was money in it.

MIKE. Tell them how much? Guess how much.

ANGELA. Hundred quid.

MIKE (*laughing*). Don't be bloody daft, go on, guess.

STACEY. It doesn't matter.

ROB. Hundred and fifty grand.

MIKE. Ten thousand. Ten thousand quid. In cash.

ANGELA. Fuck off? 'Scuse me.

MIKE. Incredible, isn't it? I mean, it doesn't compare to these bankers' bonuses but still. It's not bloody bad, is it? Not. Bad. At. All.

ANGELA. I got a gift-set from Boots from my work at Christmas. You know that Spa stuff. It's their own brand.

JULIA. Oh, that's lovely though, isn't it? Really fresh smelling.

Silence.

Let's have a photey. Come on. Everyone on the couch.

JULIA *grabs the camera.*

ANGELA. I'll take it.

JULIA. No you will not, Ang. If you take it you won't be in it. What's the point in that? (*Beat.*) Mike can take it. Robbie, come on, love… on the couch.

ROB *stands reluctantly and squashes on the end of the couch next to* ANGELA. *He puts an arm around her territorially.* MIKE *fiddles about with the camera.*

Oh, come on, don't turn it into a bloody performance.

MIKE. Hang on a minute. (*Fiddles some more.*) Okay… Now, everyone say cheese.

ANGELA. Cheese.

MIKE (*to* ROB). You can smile, Robert, you're not about to be sent down to the fucking gas chambers.

JULIA. Oh, now that's bloody disgusting.

MIKE *takes the photo, the flash goes off.*

What did you that for? I wasn't ready… take another one.

STACEY. I'll take it.

JULIA. Then you won't be in it.

STACEY. I don't want to be in it.

JULIA. Oh, Stace. She has this thing, Angela.

ROB. Vanity.

STACEY. How can it be vain if I don't want my photograph taken? (*Beat.*) Dad, sit down on the couch next to Mum.

STACEY *takes the camera and stands in front of them.* ROB *pulls* ANGELA *onto his knee and starts to kiss her neck.*

JULIA. I've got more photos of me and your father than I can fit in all my albums. (*Beat.*) Me and your father in Morecambe. Me and your father at the caravan, me and your father lagging the flaming loft –

STACEY *takes the picture. The flash goes off.*

Oh, Christ… I wasn't ready again. Let me look… I'll have my mouth wide open like a fishwife.

STACEY *shows the photograph.*

ANGELA. It's nice that, Julia.

JULIA *stands, she goes to take the camera.* MIKE *steps in the way, grabs the camera and puts in back in the case.* JULIA *sits back down, embarrassed.*

JULIA. I bet you're very photogenic, are you, Angela? (*Beat.*) I'm awful. Someone said to me once. 'For an attractive woman you don't half come out bad in photos.' *I'm* not saying I'm attractive. It was just what someone said once.

MIKE. I do think it's important though. To document special occasions. Collate all your memories. Or else what? They fly straight by and then you're in a pine box, six foot under.

JULIA. Oh, Jesus… Listen to Happy Larry. It's not a bloody wake. (*Goes over to the shelf and starts to glance along it.*) What about some music then? Stacey, let's have some music at your birthday party. What d'you fancy? (*Picking a CD out.*) Massive… Attack. Who are they then?

STACEY marches over to the CDs. She picks another, puts it into the CD player and presses play. It's Billie Holiday.

JULIA goes to MIKE and starts to dance with him. He is reluctant at first but then gives in. ROB hangs onto ANGELA tightly, she stands and drags him up. They sway stiffly from side to side.

Oh, look, we'll have to swap… Poor Stace's sitting there like a big goose-gog. Dance with your dad… I'll sit down for a bit. We can all swap round. It'll be a giggle.

JULIA sits and STACEY reluctantly stands to dance with MIKE.

JULIA watches, smiling, from the couch, inappropriately clapping her hands together. ROB tries to kiss ANGELA but she moves away towards STACEY and MIKE. She and MIKE begin to dance.

ROB looks put out. He and STACEY stand side by side. JULIA is still clapping.

Go on, you two. Have a little dance… When they were little, Angela, they used to dance together in the front room all the time. Do you remember?

ROB *and* STACEY. No.

JULIA. Oh, you do. It was so sweet. Go on, have a little dance. Go *on*.

Beat. STACEY and ROB begin to dance together, hating every second. JULIA is delighted. She stands and puts her arms around both of them, holding on tightly. ROB *and* STACEY *are pressed together awkwardly.*

They were so close, these two, Angela. They still are, really, aren't you?

STACEY *and* ROB *stay silent, trying not to look at one another.* MIKE *is enjoying his dance with* ANGELA, *showing off a little.*

Very different but close. And once you've had that bond I don't think it ever goes, does it?

JULIA *lets go of* STACEY *and* ROB *and they move away from each other awkwardly.*

ROB *goes to dance with* ANGELA *again.* MIKE *drags* JULIA *up.*

STACEY *hovers awkwardly, watching* ROB *as he clings onto* ANGELA. *Suddenly she gets up and reaches for her laptop, scrolling through she finds a song (a pop song from 1990 / 91) and presses play, turning the CD off. Everyone stops dancing.*

STACEY. Angela, remember this?

MIKE. We can't dance to that.

STACEY. Remember the dance?

Peeved, ROB *clings onto* ANGELA *as* STACEY *grabs her hand.*

I can still totally remember it.

ANGELA. Oh, you're joking, aren't you?

STACEY. Come on.

STACEY *pulls* ANGELA's *hand,* ROB *still clings tight.*

Let go of her for a minute, she's not going to evaporate.

Embarrassed, ROB *steps back, hands awkwardly in his pockets.*

Mum, start it again.

JULIA *fiddles with the laptop.*

MIKE. Don't let her go near that, for Christ's sake. She totalled my bloody Dell.

STACEY *goes to the laptop.*

ANGELA. Honestly, I won't be able to remember it.

STACEY. You will, I bet you will.

ROB. She doesn't wanna do it, Stacey.

STACEY (*shouting*). Shut up.

JULIA *laughs, embarrassed.* STACEY *presses play. She and* ANGELA *stand side by side.* STACEY *whispers an instruction to* ANGELA *and they begin a childish, slightly mechanical dance to the song, stumbling as they go.* ANGELA *looks nothing but embarrassed,* STACEY *giggles hysterically. After a bit, however, they both start to enjoy it, synchronising their steps and actually making quite an impressive effort.*

At the end, JULIA *claps and gestures for everyone to do the same.* STACEY *is particularly giddy.*

JULIA. Aww, lovely.

STACEY. It just comes back to you, doesn't it? Once you get going.

JULIA. Robbie used to do… What was it, Rob? That thing you used to like?

ROB. Hip-hop.

JULIA. Hip-hop. That's it. Funny names these things have. (*Beat.*) Break-dancing too. You used to do that too, didn't you?

ROB *nods, looking towards* ANGELA. *But she doesn't notice.*

ROB. Bit. (*Beat.*) B-boying, body-popping.

STACEY. He won a competition once.

ANGELA. Did you?

ROB. Twice. Just did battles with another crew though mostly.

STACEY. The Skelmersdale Massive.

ANGELA. Could you teach us some moves?

ROB. Yeah, it's dead simple once you've sussed it. There's four basic elements, toprock, downrock, power moves and freezes. The Indian Step's your basic toprock move, sort of like…

ROB *demonstrates slowly*.

Get that locked down then you move onto other stuff, get a bit fancy, do a G-Kick or a Master Swipe.

JULIA. He used to practise in the front room. First time I saw him I thought he was having a fit.

ANGELA. Do some then. Show us your *fancy* moves.

ROB. Nah.

ANGELA. Oh, go on.

JULIA. Come on, Robbie.

STACEY. He is good.

ROB. I'm alright.

ANGELA. Oh, go on please.

ROB *stands, he begins to limber up*.

ROB. 'Simportant to stretch. Haven't done this for years, should be wearing me trackie really.

JULIA. Do you wear tracksuits, Angela?

ANGELA. Sometimes. Only when I'm going the gym or I'm just in the house.

JULIA. Me too. We both do, don't we, Mike? On a Sunday, say. With the papers. It's just comfier, isn't it? If you don't have to go out.

Beat. ROB *continues with his stretching, it's becoming more elaborate.*

MIKE. I go to the gym.

JULIA. When do *you* go to the gym?

MIKE. When I go swimming. Took a membership when I retired. David Lloyd. Off-peak. I would've got the unlimited but there's no point. I can take guests, Stace. (*Beat.*) You could come with me when you're up discussing work stuff.

Beat.

STACEY. Yeah.

MIKE. You can hire meeting rooms.

STACEY. We won't need a meeting room –

MIKE. No, no, but you know. You can. If you want. They've got it all. Richard tipped me off. Got to keep yourself fit.

JULIA. Well, I don't know what machines you use but you'd never tell. (*Beat, to* ANGELA.) His arms are like raw chicken fillets. (*Beat.*) Do *you* wear tracksuits, Stace?

Beat. ROB *stands, ready to perform.*

STACEY. Not really.

ROB. D'you want me to do this or what?

JULIA. Sorry, Rob. Go on. We're watching.

JULIA *starts to clap her hands together and chant* ROB*'s name.*

Robbie, Robbie –

ROB. We'll have to move some stuff back.

MIKE *stays put.*

Unless you want me to kick you in the face.

They stand and move the chairs/couch back. ROB *moves the table. He stands in the space, mentally working through his 'routine'.*

I haven't done it in a while.

ROB *makes a few small moves in preparation. He takes a breath. Just as he does so,* MIKE *switches the TV on.*

What are you doing?

MIKE. News is on.

ROB *grabs the remote and switches the TV off. He takes another breath and launches into his 'routine'.*

It starts off well. He's quite adept at body-popping and ANGELA *claps and whoops as he starts on some robotics. Some awkward footwork follows which isn't quite as successful.*

Taking the plunge, he launches into a back-spin. Losing balance, he crashes into with the table, knocking over the drinks. The bottle of red wine spills onto the carpet.

MIKE *stands enraged.*

Oh, you fucking *idiot.*

ROB *rolls around on the floor, trying to disguise his pain.*

JULIA. Robbie, are you alright, love?

MIKE. Course he's alright. I'm not alright. Forty quid a bloody bottle, that was.

ROB. It was an accident.

MIKE. You're the accident. Bloody disaster zone.

ROB *stands, embarrassed. He rubs his leg.*

ROB. Think I might've broken something in me foot.

JULIA. Oh, God.

ANGELA. Can you wiggle your toes?

MIKE. He's not broken anything. He was like this when he was a kid, Angela. Attention-seeking.

JULIA. Mischievous I'd call it. Nothing more than that.

MIKE. Little get, never mind mischievous. Got away with murder. Scot-bloody-free.

ROB. Scot-free? They threw me out.

JULIA. Robbie…

MIKE. Let him, Julia. We've nothing to feel awkward about.

JULIA. We didn't throw him out, Ang.

ROB. Lucky I had mates. Would have been on the streets.

JULIA. Don't say things like that.

MIKE. Your choice, matey. Shape up or fucking ship out.

ROB. I was sixteen.

MIKE. Exactly. (*Beat.*) Old enough to know better. When I was sixteen –

STACEY. Do we have to? C'mon, it's not worth getting het up about, is it?

MIKE. I'm not getting 'het up'. I don't get 'het up'.

JULIA (*gesturing towards the carpet*). It needs white, that.

MIKE. Well, throw your fucking glass over it then. Sitting there, barking orders.

JULIA (*holds her glass protectively*). This is gin.

STACEY *runs into the kitchen. Her phone rings. She checks it and answers quickly, urgent.*

STACEY. Claire? (*Beat.*) What happened? (*Pause.*) When? (*Beat.*) Fuck. Fucking shitting *fuck.*

ANGELA *enters,* STACEY*'s tone changes immediately.* ANGELA *gets a bottle of wine from the fridge.*

Right. (*Pause.*) Right. (*Pause.*) Right. Okay. (*Long pause.*) Well… no, don't worry. No, no, don't… don't do anything. I'll call them on Monday. Okay, don't worry. It's not your fault. Have a nice weekend. (*Pause.*) Have a nice weekend. (*Pause.*) No, no, of course I'm not being / It's… Yes, no just… go home. Bye, Claire.

STACEY *cuts the call, she looks ashen.*

ANGELA. You alright?

Beat.

STACEY. Yes, yeah, it's just a work thing… boring. Problems, problems, problems. Doesn't matter really. Doesn't even… Fuck them. Forget it. (*Bats her hand dismissively.*) Just a thing with this client. Pulling the account. It's nothing. It's all part of the game.

ANGELA. What game?

STACEY. The game, you know, the general… game. I've done it myself. Friday afternoon head-fuck. Let me stew all weekend. Couple of calls Monday and it'll all be fine. (*Beat.*) It'll be fine.

ANGELA. Was it one of the film clients?

Pause.

STACEY. No, no no it was a… leisure centre.

ANGELA. Oh, well then. Least you've still got the film clients.

Silence. STACEY *nods slowly, pitiful.*

STACEY. Yes. Yeah. (*Beat.*) Thank God.

ANGELA *returns to the living room.* STACEY *sits, head in hands, before grabbing a tea towel and cleaning spray and charging into the living room. She starts to scrub the stain furiously.*

ANGELA *pours the white wine onto the stain too.*

JULIA. Oh, good girl, Angie.

JULIA *tops up her glass.*

MIKE. You'll regret that tomorrow, Julia.

JULIA. I have regretted a lot of things in my time, Mike… getting drunk has never been one of them.

MIKE. Don't we know it.

STACEY and ANGELA *are scrubbing the floor together.*
ROB *sits nursing his foot.*

That's right, Robert, you just keep an eye on things.

ROB. Hardly needs three people.

JULIA. He's hurt his foot.

MIKE. Conveniently.

JULIA. Oh, Mike, will you loosen up, for the love of God. You
get used to your own company. He used to work late quite a
lot so it feels odd really. (*Beat.*) He's unbearable... just there
constantly.

MIKE. I *said* I was working late, Julia, mostly it was so I could
stay in the office when everyone had left and have a bit of
bloody peace and quiet. I always rung though, let her know.
If she's not worrying she's not happy.

JULIA. I never worried. In fact, sometimes, when he didn't
ring, I'd secretly hope that it was because he'd been killed in
a car accident.

Silence. STACEY *and* ANGELA *stop scrubbing.*

Oh, I'm joking. How come everyone else can eff and jeff and
have a joke and I can't? Michael, hand on heart, I have never
wished you'd been killed in a car accident. I've wanted to
leave you, yes, but I can't, can I? You'd never cope. (*Beat.*)
I'll just have to wait.

STACEY *is still scrubbing.*

MIKE. How much was the deposit?

STACEY. It doesn't matter.

MIKE. It bloody does matter.

STACEY. It'll come out.

MIKE. Not with the tannin in that Shiraz. (*Beat.*) Have to get a
professional in. It'll cost a whack.

ANGELA. Can take it out of his half of the deposit.

MIKE. 'His half the deposit'? You're having a laugh, aren't you? Captain Costcutter.

STACEY (*shouting*). It's a bit of fucking wine. It'll come out.

Silence. MIKE *stares at* STACEY.

Sorry. It's just / It's not a big deal, is it?

Silence. MIKE *goes into the kitchen.* STACEY *and* ANGELA *give up on the stain.* ROB *pulls* ANGELA *onto his knee. He wraps his arms around her and leans his head against her back, squeezing her tightly.*

JULIA. He's a big baby, isn't he?

ANGELA. Easy, you'll crack me ribs.

ROB. Should eat more. You're like a little sparrow.

ROB *starts to bounce* ANGELA *up and down on his knee.*

JULIA. Thinks he can talk to me however he likes but as soon as I have a joke –

ROB. Look at how light you are. Little feather.

ANGELA. Honestly, you're getting on my nerves, stop it.

JULIA. I don't think he knows how much he hurts me sometimes.

ROB *carries on. He parts his legs so that* ANGELA *drops down onto the floor.*

He's laughing and seemingly unaware that ANGELA *is trying to stand up and move away from him. She turns around and he grabs her, not too hard, and kisses her. She responds for a moment before turning away.* ROB *continues to jiggle her up and down.*

It's supposed to be a party. We're celebrating.

ROB. We are. We're having a great time.

JULIA. But the minute I have a bit of fun. The minute I join in –

STACEY. You're pissed.

JULIA. And I wonder why that is, Stacey? I wonder why I might be just a little bit tipsy. (*Beat*.) You'd have a few spirits too many if you had to live with him.

ROB *bounces* ANGELA *up and down on his knee*.

ANGELA. Stop it now, I feel sick.

ROB. Look at how light you are.

STACEY. She doesn't want you to do that.

ANGELA *pulls away from* ROB.

ROB. Ah, don't go. Come on, I'm only having a laugh, I'll stop it now. Sit back down, here y'are, have me seat.

ROB *stands, putting his weight onto his ankle. He winces*.

JULIA. Oh, Rob, do you want a little rub, love?

ROB *sits back on the couch, clutching his leg*.

ROB. It's probably just a sprain.

JULIA. Sprains are *worse* than breaks. Remember when your father slipped, crabbing in Tenby? Wept like a baby all night. Couldn't even have a bedsheet on it. Let's have a look.

JULIA *sits beside* ROB. *He tries to put his leg on the floor but she's too quick*.

Come on, don't be a baby.

JULIA *rolls his trouser leg up to reveal an electronic tag around his ankle*.

ANGELA *spots it*.

ROB *tries to pull his trouser leg down but* JULIA *sees the tag*.

What's that, Robbie?

Beat.

STACEY. It's for jogging. Clocks up how far you've run.

ROB *is silent. He nods but stares straight ahead*.

JULIA. That's very clever. (*Beat*.) Why've you got it on in here?

ROB. Was gonna pop out in a bit. Run me dinner off.

JULIA. Well, you won't be running anything off with that sprain.

JULIA *kneels down to put her arms around* ROB. *She grabs his ankle to steady herself.*

He's a good lad, aren't you? I don't want to say 'mummy's boy' because that sounds a bit. (*Hiccups loudly.*) 'Scuse me. But he's just everso caring. Affectionate. When he was small, we used to play this game. I'd be going out to work and I'd put on my coat and get my bag and he'd be… I don't know, sitting watching TV or following me about. He did that quite a bit actually, followed me round… like a little lost lamb. So, I'd go, 'Bye, Robbie, see you later.' Then I'd walk out into the hall, open the front door and shut it but I wouldn't leave. I'd just stand there. And two seconds later he'd come flying out of the living room… his little face half-laughing, half-scared in case I really had gone without giving him a cuddle. And I'd just scoop him up in my arms and hold him tight. (*Beat.*) And that was all it was, you see, just the idea that I might go to work and not give him a hug before I left was so… preposterous, that we made in into a game. We didn't do it for very long, of course. I think we both got a bit embarrassed in the end. I'm probably doing it now. Am I doing it now? Am I embarrassing you?

ROB. No.

JULIA. I tried to do it with Stacey a couple of times but she never really latched on. I used to stand in the hall on my own. Twenty minutes I was once. Waiting. She did hold hands though. When we were out. So that was nice. (*Pause.*) I miss holding hands actually. I don't hold hands with anybody any more. Your father's are always so incredibly sweaty. Not that he wants to hold mine.

ANGELA *stares at* ROB. *He leaves the room, embarrassed.* STACEY *exits.*

JULIA *takes a gulp of her drink.* MIKE *enters. He eyes her disdainfully.*

MIKE. It's not a race. Slow down.

JULIA. Oh, slow down yourself.

ANGELA. Is it alright if I get myself another one?

JULIA. Angela, don't break my heart, lovely. You do *not* ask for anything in this house. This is our home. (*Beat.*) This is our *holiday* home. You help yourself. Doesn't she, Mike?

MIKE. Yeah. Course. Help yourself. You're our guest.

JULIA. She's not a guest. She's part of the family. Here, get a vodka and orange down your neck.

　　JULIA pours ANGELA *a drink and hands it to her.*

Let me know if it's a bit strong. We don't go out to pubs much, me and Mike, so I'm not all that good at judging. My dream come true would be to have a 'mini-bar' in the living room, wouldn't it, Mike?

MIKE. Not when there's just the two of us, Julia. It's completely unnecessary.

JULIA. *You're* completely unnecessary.

　　JULIA laughs hysterically. MIKE *stares at her.*

Oh, look at that face. He's like a wet week in Wigan sometimes, that bloody man, Ang. Miserable old so-and-so. We're supposed to be having fun and off he goes. Ranting. Upsetting everyone.

MIKE. I haven't upset anyone. Have I upset anyone?

ANGELA. You haven't upset me, Mike.

MIKE. Thank you, Angela.

　　JULIA drains her drink and walks, unsteady, to the bathroom, tapping ANGELA *on the arm.*

JULIA. Powder my nose. (*Beat, pointing to* MIKE.) Behave yourself.

　　MIKE rolls his eyes, JULIA *laughs and taps* ANGELA*'s arm again.*

Kidding. He's alright. You're alright, aren't you, Mike?

MIKE *stares ahead, silent.* JULIA *stumbles out.*

There's an awkward silence.

MIKE. He's never going to be able to do very much for you.
(*Beat.*) I know you're not asking for anything… independent
young woman… but in the future… I don't know, mortgages,
kids… that sort of thing. (*Beat.*) He's one of life's losers, is
Robert.

Silence.

It's not as harsh as it sounds. It's a roll of the dice most of the
time. Some people are winners, some people are losers.
(*Beat.*) You're a winner. Aren't yer?

ANGELA. Depends what you mean by winner.

MIKE. Good job… head on your shoulders. How many kids
from your estate are doing as well as you, eh? You might not
be on mega-bucks but relatively speaking, Angela… you are
a true winner.

ANGELA. Are you a winner, Mike?

MIKE *laughs self-consciously. He pours himself another
drink.*

MIKE. Left school when I was sixteen. Did my
apprenticeship… worked hard. Stayed out of trouble. Landed
a good job. House, kids… upgrade on the car each year. I
rely on nobody but myself and so at the risk of sounding big-
headed, yes… I am a winner.

FIVE

ROB *sits alone in the kitchen, hunched over, about to snort a line of coke.* STACEY *enters. It's a couple of seconds before she registers what* ROB *is doing.*

STACEY. For fuck's sake.

> ROB *sticks the note in his pocket and spins around, rubbing his nose furiously.*

ROB. Stace.

STACEY. What the fuck are you playing at?

ROB. What?

STACEY. Oh, don't, please / I've just seen you. I've just fucking / Mum and Dad are feet away. How can you even… What would make you want to do that when they're here? How can you even think that that's a good idea?

ROB. One tiny line, that's all. (*Beat.*) Little livener. Just gets me through all that shit.

> ROB *gestures toward the living room.*

STACEY. For fuck's sake.

ROB. I know, don't.

STACEY. I thought things were going to be different.

ROB. They are. They're different. This is / This isn't anything. I had some left over, that's all. Found it in me pocket. Been worrying in case it drops out. Thought I may as well fucking do it. Get it out the way. Get rid. Get it done.

> ROB *rubs his nose, fidgets about.*

'Snot bad actually. Thought it'd well be dud by now.

STACEY. This is fucking pathetic. What about your parole? Don't they do tests?

ROB. I can get me hands on some piss. (*Beat.*) Kid by ours.

Beat.

STACEY. What about that… thing, your *tag*. Aren't you supposed to be on a curfew?

Silence. ROB *sniffs and rubs his nose.*

Oh, fucking hell. Rob.

STACEY *sits next to him.*

ROB. I'll explain. It'll be okay. I'll tell them. Just a fucking weekend with me family. I wanted to see me family.

Silence.

Thank you.

STACEY. What for?

ROB. Just then. Covering. (*Beat.*) I think she's right, you know? Me mum. About us. It's good to see you. (*Beat.*) It's genuinely really fucking good to see you. I think we could be friends, you know?

STACEY. Do you?

ROB. I think we *should* be friends. (*Beat.*) We never speak, do we? Why d'you think that is?

STACEY. Just… get rid of that and go back in there.

ROB. I know why it is. I know it's either because I'm in the shit with something or I want money. Or both. And I pretend it's not. I pretend I'm ringing to talk or to see how you are but at the end I'll work it into the conversation about how I need something. Like I just thought of it that second. I'm so sorry about that, Stace. That's really… I wanna say passive-aggressive but I'm not sure it's in the right context. Whatever, it's not right. I'm done with all that now. The bullshit. The pretence. I'm sorry.

STACEY. It's alright, will you just put that –

ROB. It's not alright. It's fucking disgusting. You're me sister. You're me little sister. I should look after you.

STACEY. I don't need looking after.

ROB. Everyone needs looking after.

ROB puts an arm around STACEY. *Tentative at first then a proper hug.*

I love you.

No reply. ROB *clings on.*

I do. I love you. I'm gonna pay you back every single penny you've ever lent me.

STACEY. I don't want your money. You haven't got any anyway.

ROB. I know but I will have, I swear. I know we're completely different and we don't get on but… I love you. (*Beat.*) I'm dead proud of you.

ROB takes the coke out of his pocket.

Watch that door for us, will you?

STACEY *watches as* ROB *starts cutting two lines of coke out onto the table.*

I'm gonna come to London and stay with you. We can go out for tea or something, yeah? Go and see a show. How long you been in London now?

STACEY. Twelve years. This is fucking ridiculous.

ROB. I know, it's disgusting. I have *never* been to see you. In *twelve* years. (*Beat.*) Don't have to worry about putting us up. I'll get a hotel.

STACEY. *This* is fucking ridiculous.

ROB picks up the note and snorts a line.

ROB. D'you think she got on to it?

STACEY....

ROB. Angela. Have I fucked it up?

STACEY....

ROB. I reckon it'll be okay. I'm glad, y'know? I'm fucking /
It's all... out there now, isn't it? No more lies. She gets me.
She fucking gets me. She understands. (*Beat.*) She
understands me.

Silence.

Honestly thought this'd be dead by now. It's fucking lovely.
What d'you reckon then? London. It'll be like a little
holiday. Like a wotsit... city break. I'll bring Angela. (*Beat.*)
I'm sorry, Stacey. I am so sorry. Things are gonna be
different. Every penny, I swear. (*Beat.*) I wanted to come. I
wanted to be here. To see you.

STACEY. Did you?

ROB. Yeah. Course. That's *fucking* strong that.

> ROB *stands. He hesitates before grabbing hold of* STACEY
> *and hugging her again.*

I love you.

> ROB *disappears outside.* STACEY *looks completely lost, she
> looks at the line of coke on the table and then towards the
> door. She hesitates before sitting down and picking up the
> rolled-up note and quickly snorting the line.*

> STACEY *throws her head back.* ANGELA *enters.* STACEY
> *jumps up wiping the table with one hand and sticking the
> note in her pocket with the other.* ANGELA *sits down at the
> kitchen table and lights a cigarette.*

STACEY. Can I have one?

> STACEY *takes a cigarette.* ANGELA *lights it for her.*

ANGELA. Thought you didn't smoke.

STACEY. I don't.

STACEY *inhales the cigarette, laughs nervously.*

Think I'm not quite used to it yet. You being here.

ANGELA. What did he do?

STACEY. I think you should talk to him.

ANGELA. Nothing to do with kids, is it?

STACEY. Fuck's sake. No. (*Beat.*) He's not / Jesus.

ANGELA. Some people are. And they haven't got it written on
    their foreheads. Remember Oaksey, ran the corner shop by
    me mum's? Why d'you think he was always giving us penny
    chews? He was grooming us, wasn't he?

STACEY. He's *not* a paedophile.

ANGELA. Long as it's not kids or violence.

STACEY. He's not violent.

    Silence. ANGELA *nods.*

You must have realised before now.

ANGELA. No.

STACEY. Aren't you… angry?

    ANGELA *shrugs.*

ANGELA. Only met him on Wednesday.

STACEY. Wednesday? As in –

ANGELA. Day before yesterday, yeah. Seventies night at that
    place that keeps changing its name, opposite the Conny. You
    wouldn't know it, would you? Anyway, there.

STACEY. On… Wednesday?

ANGELA. Yeah.

STACEY. You don't even know him.

ANGELA. Not really.

    Silence.

STACEY. Why are you here?

Silence. ANGELA *stares at* STACEY.

ANGELA. Your ears have closed over.

ANGELA *reaches up and feels* STACEY*'s earlobe.*

Can still feel the little knot though.

ANGELA *pulls her hand away. She dips it into her drink and pulls out a cube of ice, presses it against* STACEY*'s ear.*

Hold that there.

ANGELA *takes out one of her huge dangly earrings. She hands* STACEY *a drink.*

Have a swig of that and hold your breath.

STACEY. Oh no –

ANGELA. Go on. It won't hurt.

STACEY *takes a swig.* ANGELA *moves quickly, deftly taking the ice cube away and plunging the earring into* STACEY*'s ear.* STACEY *yelps.*

ANGELA *holds her make-up mirror up. She stands behind* STACEY, *looking over her shoulder.*

Suits you.

STACEY *takes the mirror and looks.*

I brought something for you.

STACEY *puts the mirror down.* ANGELA *digs in her pocket and pulls out a strip of photo-booth photos. She hands it to* STACEY. STACEY *takes it and stares at it for a long time.*

STACEY. I can't believe you kept this.

ANGELA. Found it in me box.

STACEY. You've got a box? I've got a box. I kept everything.

Beat.

That was a brilliant day.

ANGELA. Wasn't it?

Beat.

STACEY. Best day of my life.

Silence.

I turned up, you know. I turned up at the station. Waited all morning. Got worried, thought something had happened to you.

ANGELA. Sorry.

STACEY. Then I just thought... Nah. She doesn't want to. She's changed her mind. Logical thing would've been to just go to yours but you don't do logic, do you? That age. If someone did that now, if someone let me down. Like that. First thing I'd do is go round to see them. Ask them what's going on. But when you're a kid, it's so much easier to pretend you don't care. But I did care. I really really cared. (*Beat.*) Daft. Kids' stuff. Dunno why I'm telling you now.

STACEY *laughs nervously.*

Blow the bloody dust off, Stacey. (*Pause.*) It's funny, isn't it? Things you plan when you're that age. Everything's so... *dramatic.* (*Beat.*) I wrote Mum and Dad a letter. Posted it. I thought, by the time it arrives we'll be there and it'll be too late for them to do anything about it. I slept in the living room that night so I could get there first when the postman came. Rip it up.

ANGELA. Why was it Blackpool?

STACEY. Said your cousin could get us jobs in the fair.

ANGELA. Oh, aye. The waltzers.

STACEY. I wouldn't have stuck that more than a day. Bloody hell. Couldn't go in the car without spewing if we went round the roundabout. I'm still like that.

ANGELA. I was gonna come. I wanted to.

STACEY. Did you?

ANGELA. Yeah.

STACEY. Funny, isn't it? Kids.

Silence.

We should do it now. Go somewhere. Sod bloody Blackpool. Let's go somewhere hot.

STACEY *laughs nervously.*

Couldn't we though?

ANGELA. It's difficult. Getting away from the shop.

STACEY. Yeah, yeah, of course. And it would be tricky for me actually. (*Beat.*) With work.

ANGELA. I've booked for Portugal in October anyway.

STACEY. Lovely, that'll be / I haven't been but I've heard it's very… nice. Hot. In October. (*Pause.*) I missed you. (*Beat.*) I did, I missed you so much. I still do in a funny sort of way. I get this sort of ache. Actually. When I think about you.

STACEY *stares at* ANGELA. *She leans forward and kisses her.*

ANGELA *pulls away, stubs her cigarette out then leaves.* STACEY *studies the photograph.*

SIX

JULIA *is slumped on the couch.* STACEY *and* ANGELA *are sitting away from each other as* MIKE *puffs on his cigar.*

ROB *enters, even more wired than before. His hands cupped together.*

ROB. Someone get us a glass.

MIKE. What did your last slave die of?

ROB. Can't open me hands, can I? Mum, go on.

    JULIA *is starting to drift off.*

JULIA. What, love?

    ROB *gives up. He goes into the kitchen and returns with a butterfly in a jam jar. He hands it to* MIKE.

ROB. Peace offering.

    JULIA *sits up, takes another sip of her drink.*

JULIA. Aww. They used to do this, Ang, years ago. Had a little net, didn't you? They'd go out, the pair of them. Loved it, didn't you?

    MIKE *inspects the butterfly.*

MIKE. Meadow Brown that.

ROB. Gatekeeper.

MIKE. How much?

ROB. I don't wanna bet. I know I'm right.

MIKE. Then you've got nothing to lose, have you? (*Beat.*) Twenty quid.

ROB. No point.

MIKE. There's no point if, you know, you're wrong. If you think you're right then there's absolutely a point. You get twenty quid.

ROB. It's a Gatekeeper.

MIKE *gets a twenty-pound note from his wallet. He lays it on the table.*

MIKE. Meadow Brown. Get the book.

ROB. I don't need the book.

MIKE. Put your money where your mouth is then. Julia, get the book.

JULIA. They're bloody awful, these two, Angela. One says black the other says white. I don't see what difference it makes.

MIKE. It's a bit of fun. We're having *fun.* It's a *party.* Did you bring the book?

JULIA. Course I brought it. I had to bring it, didn't I? I don't know what the obsession with the bloody book's all about. Why you can't just go for a walk and appreciate the surroundings without having to identify the make of every bloody creature and plant we come across, I've got no idea.

MIKE. You don't say 'make', Julia. It's the 'type', the 'species'.

JULIA. Oh, piss off, Mike.

ROB. Mum, get the book.

JULIA. World War Three over a bloody moth.

JULIA *gets the book from her bag, flicks through.* MIKE *takes it off her.*

MIKE. You won't be able to *differentiate*, Julia.

JULIA. I'll bloody differentiate you if you're not careful.

MIKE *flicks through, studying the pages. He suddenly lets out a huge satisfied shout.*

MIKE. Ha. Meadow Brown. Thank you. Twenty quid, Robert, please.

STACEY. You've proved your point, Dad. You don't need twenty pounds.

MIKE. Course I don't need twenty quid. It's not about the twenty quid. Little lesson, mate. Don't bet with what you haven't got. Tell you what. Do it in instalments, eh? Quid a week.

ROB. I'll give you twenty quid. I've got it here. Can fucking choke on it.

JULIA. Now, oi, this is what I mean about gambling. It always escalates into something ugly.

MIKE. It does if you haven't got the money to gamble with in the first place.

ROB. I've got the money. I've got the money. I've got the fucking money.

JULIA. It all comes back to the bloody money. Twenty pounds. Is it worth all this for twenty pounds?

MIKE. It's not the money, Julia. It's about… honour.

ROB. Who d'you think you are? The fucking Godfather?

JULIA. Who's any good with Pictionary?

MIKE. We don't have to play games all the time, Julia. We're adults. We can talk. We can *chat*. Discuss things.

JULIA. What was that one we used to do in the car? Stace, what was it? The singing one.

JULIA *thinks.* ROB *and* MIKE *eyeball each other.*

You had to make up your own words to a tune that everyone knew. We did it like a competition. Whoever won got a little prize.

MIKE. Stacey always won. Rob's never been any good at that sort of thing. You've got your left-brain types and your right-brain types. Unfortunately, he's neither.

MIKE *laughs*.

JULIA. Usually I'd sneak them both a prize cos it's not fair, is it? With kids.

MIKE. See, I don't agree with that but –

JULIA. Rob's more sporty, aren't you? He's got this thing, Mike. Tells him how far he's run. (*Beat.*) What's it called?

STACEY. A pedometer.

ROB *nods slowly*.

JULIA. Thing I don't understand is why anyone needs to know how far they've run. Why can't you just go for a nice jog and not worry about it.

MIKE. Because it's about competition, Julia. Being better than the man next to you.

JULIA. It looks everso bulky, Rob. Does it chafe your ankle?

ROB *shakes his head nervously*. MIKE *looks up*.

How far have you done on it up to now then? Richard's son Daniel's forever flying past our window, isn't he, Mike?

Silence.

He seems very driven. I bet he's got a pedometer.

MIKE *kneels on the floor in front of* ROB *and pulls his trouser legs up*. MIKE *stares at the tag then sits back down in the chair*.

Stace, what did that peanut song go like?

STACEY. I don't know.

JULIA. Oh, you do. It was so catchy, Angela, we used to sing it all the time.

Silence.

STACEY (*singing to the tune of 'My Darling Clementine'*).
Found a peanut, found a peanut, found a peanut on the floor,
just now I found a peanut, found a peanut on the floor.

JULIA (*clapping*). Aww, lovely. That was it.

> ANGELA *pulls the twenty quid from her pocket then produces another twenty and a ten. She hands them to* MIKE.

MIKE. Oh, come on now. Don't go overcompensating for him. He might be alright with you stumping up for his debts but I'm not. Short arms, long bloody pockets, that's his problem.

ANGELA. I owe it to you, Mike.

MIKE. You don't owe me anything.

ANGELA. Didn't think you remembered.

STACEY. Remembered what?

ANGELA. I met your dad once. He drove through our estate in his nice car. Was it a Jag?

JULIA. It was a Jag. Mike, you never said you met Ang? I didn't even know they were pals. She didn't have many pals, did you, Stace?

ANGEL. Fifty quid. I want you to have it back.

> ANGELA *holds the money out towards* MIKE *again*.

STACEY. What's going on?

MIKE. I don't want it.

ANGELA. I'm not trying to make you feel uncomfortable.

STACEY. What are you talking about?

ANGELA. Take it.

MIKE. Daft bet. All getting our knickers in a twist over nothing.

> ANGELA *is still holding the money out*.

ANGELA. I'm not getting my knickers in a twist. I owe you fifty quid.

JULIA. We pay per room so it's no difference whether you came or not. Is it, Mike? And honestly he will get offended if you keep on about it.

ANGELA. It's nothing to do with the fucking bet. I owe you fifty quid.

JULIA (*laughing nervously*). Ooh…

Silence.

MIKE. It wasn't anything personal. I didn't know anything about you. Your life.

ANGELA. No, you didn't.

MIKE. Fifteen's a tricky age. Think they know it all. She was going through a lot at the time. (*Beat.*) I was just looking out for my daughter.

ANGELA. Keeping her on the straight and narrow. Keep her away from the scumbags.

MIKE. I did what I thought was right at the time. You said yourself before, some of those kids on that estate. I didn't know you.

ANGELA. Didn't get the chance. Paying me off.

MIKE. Fifty quid, for Christ's sake. If I'd wanted to pay you off…

STACEY. You bribed her?

MIKE. It wasn't a *bribe*.

STACEY. You *paid* her not to be my friend.

ANGELA. I only took it because I felt embarrassed. Then afterwards. I couldn't return it. Didn't know where you lived. Anyway, here it is. I've come to pay it back.

MIKE. She was being bullied.

STACEY. Not by *her*.

MIKE. *He* started going off the rails. We had police knocking on the door and everything. Julia's nerves were shot to bloody pieces. Then Richard from next-door-but-one mentions in passing about seeing Stacey with one of the / With *you*. (*Beat.*) Bloody head starts working overtime. Protective father, that's all.

STACEY. Protective? Are you serious? Is that what you where doing when I was begging you to let me move schools? *Protecting* me?

MIKE. I think we should all just take a breather… calm down.

STACEY. Day after fucking day of *torture*.

MIKE. Oh, come on, raking up the past, it does no good, no bloody good at all.

ANGELA. Take the money then and we can move on. Forget about it.

STACEY. The only thing I had, the only fucking person who helped me through it and you paid her off?

MIKE. I didn't mean to… hurt anyone.

ANGELA. You didn't hurt me.

MIKE. Good.

ANGELA. I had this favourite teacher in school. Mrs Jones. She used to hand out sweets and let us watch *Sesame Street*. Then I heard her talking about parents' evening, how she dreaded talking to me dad cos he stunk of piss. *That* was hurtful. I couldn't lift him and they only sent someone round once a week.

MIKE. …

ANGELA. You didn't hurt me cos I don't know you. You offended me. You embarrassed me. But you didn't hurt me. *(Beat.)* I want you to take it.

Silence. MIKE *picks up the notes from the arm of the chair. He puts them in his wallet and sits back in his chair.*

JULIA *gets the book.* ROB *takes the twenty-pound note that* MIKE *has laid on the table and covers the Gatekeeper with it, crushing it in his fist.* JULIA *takes the book. She flicks through and finds the entry for the Gatekeeper. She opens up the note and examines the squashed butterfly.*

JULIA. 'The Gatekeeper. Note the two white spots in the forewing. Meadow Brown only has one white spot and is overall less brightly coloured.' You *are* right, Rob. It is a Gatekeeper. (*Beat.*) Well done, love.

JULIA *goes to pour herself another drink.* MIKE *tries to take the glass away.*

Fuck off, Mike. (*Beat.*) Forty years of marriage. You get less than half that for bloody murder.

MIKE. I don't think everyone wants to hear about our marital problems, Julia.

JULIA. It's not the same as when you're young, is it? Not like these two lovebirds. And Stace and David.

STACEY. I've left him.

JULIA. No, you haven't. What did you do that for?

STACEY. I don't love him. I haven't loved him for a long time. I find him incredibly boring.

JULIA. Oh, come on, he's not *that* boring. Has he been playing around with someone in work?

STACEY. No.

JULIA. Because I found a receipt once, Mike? This is before internet and mobiles and the 1471. Years ago. Before he got all his ear-hair. I found this receipt for this restaurant that I'd always wanted him to take me to. And I'm not proud of it but I jumped straight to the wrong conclusion. Hacked all his best shirts to pieces with the pinking shears. And it was nothing in the end. A load of fuss and bother over nothing. And d'you know? Thinking about it. In retrospect. If you looked me in the eyes now, Mike, and said you'd taken another woman out for the night, I'm not saying I'd condone it but I honestly don't think I'd be that bothered.

STACEY. It isn't anybody else. I'm just not happy.

MIKE. Happy?

STACEY. Yes, *happy*. I'm not *happy* with him, I want to be *happy*. That's all. What's the fucking problem? Is that not in Mike's fucking 'Winners' Rulebook'? Are not you allowed to be with someone just because they make you happy? Or is that for fucking losers?

Pause.

MIKE. Will we see him again?

STACEY. I doubt it. Why would you?

MIKE. Thought he might have been in touch. Say goodbye.

STACEY. He thinks you're a prick.

Silence.

JULIA. Is it a relief though, Stace? Is it like a weight off your shoulders?

STACEY. Yeah.

JULIA. Well, that's the main thing. Let's have a toast. To Stacey being happy on her own.

ANGELA (*raising her glass*). To Stacey being happy.

ROB *raises his can of Guinness.* MIKE *sips his whiskey, refusing to join in.* JULIA *drains her glass.*

JULIA *picks up a newspaper from the floor by the chair.*

JULIA (*reading from the paper*). 'I am learning to ask questions and let go of wanting answers. Relevant questions are like brooms that sweep the mind and create a clean space. The mind needs clean space. Answers enter clean space. When I am too focused on answers, I lose them.' (*Beat.*) I read 'Thought for the Day' in the newspaper, Angela. They're usually very good but I'm not quite sure what that one means today. What do you think that one means?

MIKE. I'll give your mind some fucking clean space. Reading this fucking shit day after day. (*Beat.*) Stop pouring gin down your neck, that'll give your mind some space. Go to fucking AA. Talk your bullshit there.

Beat. JULIA *reads.*

JULIA. 'Amidst the earthquakes of unexpected situations, the hurricanes of unreasonable behaviour, when fortune strikes against me, I will remain unmoved, knowing that finally, all will be – '

MIKE *stands and snatches the paper out of* JULIA'*s hand.*

STACEY *rushes at him, trying to pull the paper out of his hands.* MIKE *snatches it back.*

Leave it, love, he's depressed.

STACEY *sits back down, weary.*

MIKE (*ripping the paper to shreds*). Depressed my arse. She's round the fucking twist, your mother. She thinks I'm *depressed* because I don't want to sit there talking about fucking disease-ridden animals day in, day out. She thinks I'm *depressed* because I like my own space. Do you know what she bought me the other day? Fucking packet of crayons. Now that *is* enough to make me depressed. Grown man, sitting there, fucking… colouring-in. I am perfectly content. I can just do without her quoting nonsense at me left right and fucking centre – 'Do you know why they call today, the present? Because it's a *gift.*' Tell you what'd be a bloody gift. Five minutes' fucking peace. Twenty-four hours a day. Driving me mad. Early retirement, what a joke that is. Taking it easy. Chance'd be a fucking fine thing.

Beat.

JULIA. Early retirement. That is a bloody joke. Can you imagine him taking early retirement? He'd be going till he dropped if he could. Early retirement, you bloody wish, Michael.

MIKE. Julia, shut up.

JULIA. No I won't shut up. I will not fucking shut up. Okay? (*Beat.*) They got rid, packed him off early because he kept cocking up left right and bloody centre. Liability they called him –

MIKE. That is a lie –

JULIA. I read it on the computer, on your emails. A bloody
liability. Couldn't keep up. Course they dressed it up, offered
him a parcel –

MIKE. A package.

JULIA. Made it sound like they're doing him a big favour after
all his 'years of service', but that's what it was… He couldn't
hack it. Wasn't good enough. Past it. There's all these young
ones now, the Luke Taylors. They don't want the likes of him
getting in the way.

Silence. MIKE *sits down on the couch, pathetic. Done.*

ROB *holds a hand out to him.* MIKE *looks at it for a moment
before renewed anger bubbles up. He pushes* ROB*'s hand
away hard.*

MIKE. This is perfect, isn't it? Isn't this fucking perfect? How
long have you waited for this? How happy does this make
you?

ROB. It doesn't.

MIKE. Oh, come on, don't give me all that shit. Pack it in now.
You haven't been to fucking Thailand, so drop the new-age
bollocks. Get your head out of cloud-bloody-cuckoo-land
and down to the Job Centre, sell the fucking *Big Issue* if you
have to. You're not kidding anyone.

ROB. Neither are you. You're the loser. You're the fucking
loser.

MIKE *rushes at* ROB *who puts his arms around him tightly,
holding him.* MIKE *stops struggling, his arms by his side.
They stay like this for a few moments before* ROB *lets go.*

JULIA. Will it be okay, Robbie?

Beat.

ROB. Yeah. It'll be alright, Mum. Everything'll be alright.

MIKE *snorts derisively.*

STACEY *stands and walks calmly towards* MIKE. *She whacks him hard across the face. He stands in shocked silence. She hits him again repeatedly.* ROB *pulls her away.*

MIKE (*to* STACEY). I'd think very carefully if I was you.

STACEY. Or what?

MIKE....

STACEY. I don't want your *help*. If that's what you're on about. I don't want it. You can keep it.

MIKE. You won't get very far without it.

STACEY. I don't think that's true actually.

MIKE. I'd say it –

STACEY. I don't care what you'd say. I do not fucking care what you'd say. You stick it up your fucking backside.

MIKE. When you have kids –

STACEY. Oh, don't start with that. Don't start with that *shit* –

MIKE. Then... you'll understand.

STACEY. I don't fucking need children to understand. I don't even want kids. I understand. I fucking well understand. You've ruined us... D'you know that? You've fucking ruined us.

Beat. ROB *puts an arm around* STACEY.

JULIA. God only knows what Angela's going to go and tell her family about us. She's the one from Brookvale, we're the ones that end up acting like bloody animals.

STACEY *lets out a frustrated scream. She grabs the framed picture of the four of them, throws it on the floor and stamps on it before balling herself up on the couch.*

Silence.

JULIA *gets down on her hands and knees, brushing the shattered glass away from the photo and removing it from the frame.*

ANGELA. I'm gonna go.

ROB. Yeah, c'mon, babe, let's go.

ANGELA. On me own.

Pause.

ROB. I'm coming with you. I'm not letting you –

ANGELA. Sorry.

ROB. Please. Please don't –

ANGELA. No.

ROB. Please. Angela.

STACEY. She doesn't fucking want you. You don't even know
    her. He doesn't even know her, he only fucking met her on
    Wednesday.

ROB. Shut the fuck up.

JULIA. I give up.

    ANGELA *goes to leave.* ROB *grabs her arm.*

ROB. Let me come with you.

ANGELA. I don't want you to.

ROB. Please.

STACEY. Let go of her.

ROB. We can get first class back.

ANGELA. I don't want you to come with me.

ROB (*shouts at* STACEY). Look what you've fucking done now.

ANGELA. It's nothing to do with her.

JULIA. Let her go, love.

    ROB *stands in front of the door.* STACEY *sinks onto the
    couch.* JULIA *sits down, putting an arm around her.*
    STACEY *starts to cry.* JULIA *takes some small glass bottles
    out of her pocket and lines them up on the table.*

You should have some of these. They're my special
remedies. I take them every day. I only started on Tuesday
but there's definitely been improvements. You get a little
chart from the chemist and you match your problems to the
remedy. You can take up to seven at a time. They're very
specific. (*Beat.*) You are shy or you feel anxious about
something, Mimulus. You feel extreme terror about
something, Rock Rose. Your talkativeness leads to
loneliness, Heather. You feel anxious about someone else's
safety, Red Chestnut. You feel guilty or blame yourself,
Pine. Your mind is running over the same thing, White
Chestnut. You feel tired after making an effort, Olive. You
feel wounded, jealous, spiteful, or want revenge, Holly.
You feel despair when there's no hope left, Sweet
Chestnut.

Silence.

ROB *moves away from the door. He sits against the wall to
the side of it.* ANGELA *leaves.*

JULIA *gestures for* MIKE *to come and sit at the other side
of* STACEY. *He does so, stiffly putting his arm around her
shoulder.*

Come on now, Stace. We're all here together.

STACEY *nods.* JULIA *gently lifts* STACEY*'s head and puts
a cotton hanky against her cheek.*

There you go. Soaking my arm... You used to do that when
you were small. Tears the size of Christmas baubles. I've got
this silk blouse and it's still got a water mark on it now. I
could dye it probably but I don't mind. (*Beat.*) I like it. I like
wearing your little tears.

ROB *sits, still slumped.*

We're leaving Robbie out. Rob love, come and sit over here
with us.

MIKE *hesitates then moves along slightly, allowing room for*
ROB.

That's it. Come on, Robbie. In the middle for the golden fiddle. That's it, come on. (*Beat.*) We're all here.

ROB *reluctantly sits between* MIKE *and* STACEY. MIKE *raises his arm awkwardly and puts it around* ROB.

They stay like this.

The End.